A Soul Set Free

Vol. 1

by
KJ GOFORTH

Gotham Books

30 N Gould St.
Ste. 20820, Sheridan, WY 82801
https://gothambooksinc.com/

Phone: 1 (307) 464-7800

© 2023 *KJ GoForth*. All rights reserved.

No part of this book may be reproduced, stored in a retrieval system, or transmitted by any means without the written permission of the author.

Published by Gotham Books (December 13, 2023)

ISBN: 979-8-88775-790-2 (H)
ISBN: 979-8-88775-788-9 (P)
ISBN: 979-8-88775-789-6 (E)

Because of the dynamic nature of the Internet, any web addresses or links contained in this book may have changed since publication and may no longer be valid.

Contents

SPIRITUAL SLAVERY 1

TIMELINE AND SHADOW ASPECTS 4

Deception Through Altered Reality 11

Perceptions Over Intuition 18

    The sick and sad reality of religion: 23

    What power fears: 25

    Conflict: 26

    Awake but not fully aware. 33

    Twisted lies vs. truth verses 35

    What moved by the men made holy spirit means from my prospective: 36

    Spiritual crisis-You are the canoe. Life is the river (past), stream(present) or pond (now). 42

    When possessions define us, our character becomes flawed - Philanthropy 44

    Rising awareness: 51

    An intriguing proposition arises: 56

    Enemy 87

    Self 87

    Your delicate light sparks my own flame 95

    If love becomes a snare, the world faces turmoil. 95

    Purpose: End Dark Reign 101

How I See the World of Disfunction 108

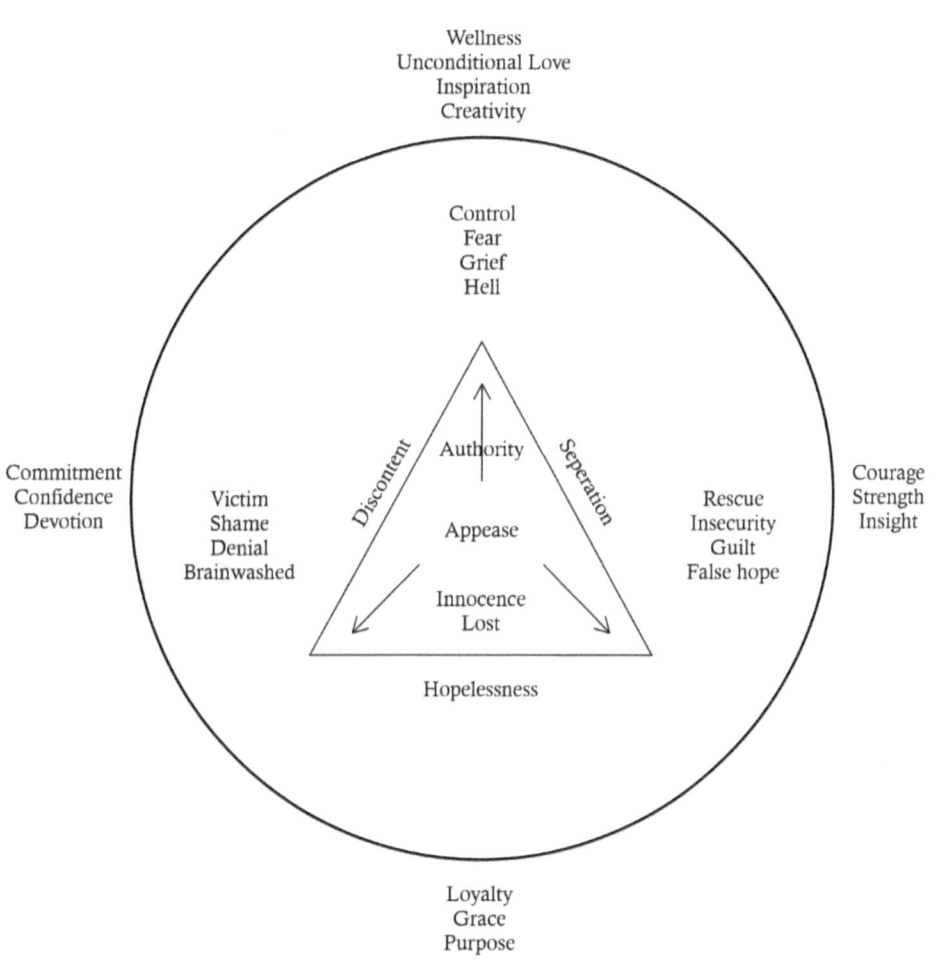

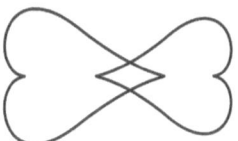 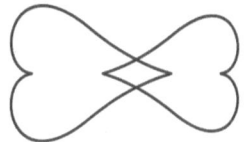

SPIRITUAL SLAVERY

While I may not possess the credentials of a history scholar or theologian, it is undeniable that throughout the annals of time, world religions have played a significant role in shaping the course of history. It is through the lens of religious ideologies that conflicts have often arisen, causing bloodshed and strife. Unfortunately, as history unfolds, we witness a disheartening pattern of repetition, where the lessons of the past remain unlearned, and humanity finds itself mired in conflicts fueled by divisive attitudes and religious dogmas. This recurring cycle points to a deep-rooted problem within our collective consciousness.

The repetition of history's conflicts signals a lack of growth and a failure to heed the wisdom of our predecessors. It is disheartening to witness the continued descent into conflict, followed by the chaos and distraction that engulfs societies, ultimately allowing religion to hold supreme power. This pattern indicates a detachment from the lessons that history should have taught us, a failure to evolve beyond our divisive tendencies and embrace the principles of compassion, understanding, and tolerance. To break free from this cycle, we must embark on a collective journey of introspection and growth. We must acknowledge that the true essence of religion lies

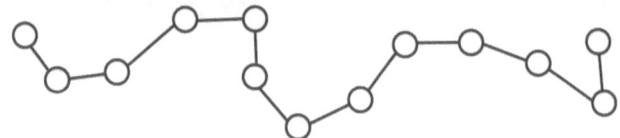

in fostering unity, love, and a connection to the divine. By transcending the narrow confines of dogma and embracing the universal values that underpin all faiths, we can forge a new path forward. It is only through a conscious effort to learn from history's mistakes, nurture a genuine understanding of one another, and cultivate a society founded on compassion and empathy that we can rise above the repetitive patterns that have plagued our past.

Within the confines of these pages, I acknowledge that the words contained herein may elicit shock and perhaps even anger among certain readers. However, it is imperative to understand that my intent is not to provoke discord or enrage, but rather to ignite conversations and inspire profound thought. For over four decades, I have struggled to suppress a gift that now demands to be shared. No longer shall I withhold it. The essence of this work lies in fostering open dialogue and breaking free from the constraints of conformity and dogma. It is an exploration of the lost translations and deliberate alterations that have permeated the pages of a revered tome, casting a lasting shadow upon humanity.

I humbly submit that the content of this work may challenge established beliefs and question long-held truths. In the pursuit of knowledge, we must acknowledge that translations can be flawed, manipulated, and distorted. It is through

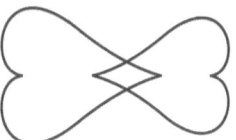 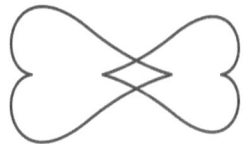

this recognition that we uncover the profound impact these alterations have had on shaping the power dynamics within religious institutions. By shedding light on these discrepancies, we empower ourselves to embark on a journey of discovery and contemplation, free from the confines of imposed authority and rigid doctrine. It is my sincere hope that by engaging in these conversations, we can collectively strive for a more nuanced and authentic understanding of our shared human experience.

In confronting the discrepancies and manipulations that have influenced religious texts, we take a courageous step toward reclaiming our own power and emancipating our collective consciousness. It is only through the liberation of thought and the fearless pursuit of truth that we can begin to heal the wounds inflicted by distorted interpretations. By encouraging open discourse and inspired contemplation, we invite the opportunity for personal growth and the dismantling of oppressive structures that have hindered our progress as a society. Let us embark on this journey with humility, seeking a more enlightened perspective that honors the essence of our shared humanity.

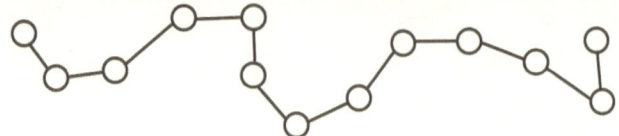

TIMELINE AND SHADOW ASPECTS

As a collective species, we often find ourselves trapped in the clutches of regrets and haunted by the specters of past traumas. The longer we allow these burdens to reverberate within our very being, the more they erode our precious energy. However, there is solace to be found in the stillness of the mind and the goodness of the heart, for it is within this sacred space that we can begin to perceive life through a renewed lens, with a fresh attitude and perspective. As we witness the alignment of our healthy desires with the unfolding tapestry of existence, it feels as if miracles surround us at every turn.

The journey towards embracing such profound miracles begins by delving into the depths of our own souls and cultivating deeper levels of admiration, gratitude, and respect for ourselves. In the tender nurturing of our own spirits, these transformative attitudes flourish, and in turn, naturally spill over to touch the lives of others. However, it is crucial to acknowledge that fear has been a formidable barrier preventing the unfettered growth of unconditional love upon our beloved mother earth. The memories imprinted within the collective consciousness, the hive mind of humanity, bear witness to the scarcity of such

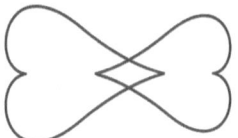 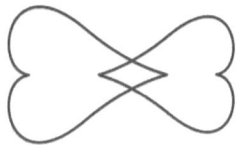

boundless love. And yet, nestled within the core of our being, lies the potential to redefine our individual and collective realities.

Imagine, if you will, that each of us is akin to an antenna, capable of receiving and transmitting energy from the vast and timeless repository known as the Akashic Records. To tap into this profound source of wisdom and experience, we must attune ourselves to the correct vibrational frequency and harmonize our very essence with the symphony of the universe. Through this alignment, we can unlock the floodgates of infinite love and boundless knowledge that the Akashic Records hold. It is a matter of being in tune, riding the wave of elevated consciousness, and embracing our inherent interconnectedness with all aspects of existence.

In essence, our journey as a species hinges upon our ability to release the weight of regrets and break free from the chains of past traumas. When we cultivate a tranquil mind and a compassionate heart, miracles become woven into the fabric of our everyday lives. As we deepen our self admiration, gratitude, and respect, we nurture a fertile ground from which these transformative attitudes emanate. Let us acknowledge the pervasive influence of fear, which has stifled the growth of unconditional love throughout history. Yet, within our very essence lies the potential to transcend these limitations, for each of us

possesses the innate power to receive and transmit energy from the vast Akashic Records. Through a conscious alignment of our vibrational frequencies, we can tap into the limitless wisdom and love that reside within the cosmic tapestry. May we embark on this journey of self-discovery and collective transformation, embracing the miracles that await us and sharing our newfound attitudes with the world.

As attitudes evolve and perspectives undergo transformative shifts, the various facets of personal growth gain momentum, resulting in an accelerated positive change in the collective energy. This shift is ignited by the individual's journey of self-discovery, where the realization of unity within oneself becomes a catalyst for profound transformation. Through the lens of oneness, the profound eyes of creation are unveiled, illuminating the interconnectedness of all existence. It is within this transformative process that the growth of our species finds its true path, guided by the principles of unity and shared consciousness.

In this journey towards collective growth, the conventional structures and organizations that once proclaimed authority and enforced conformity have lost their grip. Instead, the values of sovereignty, respect, honesty, trust, courage, and strength emerge as victorious beacons of light. These qualities reflect the

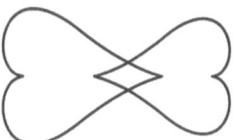 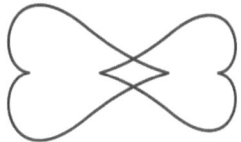

essence of our collective fight, a battle that each individual undertakes alone, yet united as one. It is through embracing our inherent sovereignty and standing tall in our authentic power that we pave the way forward, fostering a society grounded in mutual respect and shared values.

The path towards a harmonious and enlightened future lies in recognizing the strength of our unified existence. As we stand together, hand in hand, we transcend the limitations of division and separation. It is through the recognition of our interconnectedness that we unlock the true potential of our species. Let us march forward with courage, embracing the transformative power of unity, and forging a future where the echoes of sovereignty, respect, honesty, trust, courage, and strength resound in every aspect of our shared existence.

Within the realm of knowing lies the essence of being. To possess true knowledge is to transcend the boundaries of mere existence and embark upon a transformative journey of growth. It is through this process of becoming that we strive to achieve greatness, for greatness is the culmination of our endeavors and the realization of our fullest potential. In the pursuit of greatness, we unlock the vast realm of possibility, where all boundaries dissolve and the extraordinary becomes attainable.

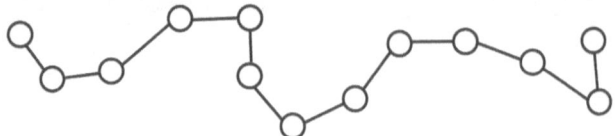

Personal notes:

We are and always have been as one to all things.

By getting out of your own way, growth change and truth is attained.

When false ego dies, transcendental ego flourishes.

In order to get love we must give love without strings.

The union to self and planet is our most sacred gift.

True passion loves itself.

A committed mind to a loving heart lift us from darkness.

Agendas come and go. Love is the ever present constant, for without love all things would be perished.

When the wars are over, love wins.

When our interpersonal wars won, we are lifted by love.

Exploration of the mind free's up the heart.

Accountability of acts and thoughts change prospective.

Is it not ironic that certain significant Christian holidays coincide with equinox cycles and involve acts of worship? On another note, some traditions perpetuate the idea of a fictional character, like a

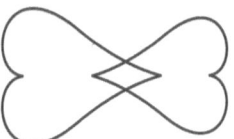 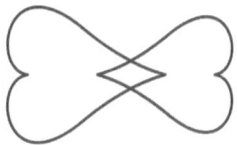

jolly man in a red suit, who watches over us throughout the year. These manipulative tactics, often targeted at children, can be disheartening when we contemplate the deeper implications. Upon introspection and examining the meaning behind various traditions, I have become disenchanted with certain practices.

I am troubled by the way organizations have historically influenced and controlled masses through emotional manipulation, instilling dogmas that have often led to mistreatment and suffering. The misuse of religious beliefs to justify suffering and pain is particularly distressing. It feels like such messages only serve the interests of criminal enterprises, undermining the true essence of compassion and understanding.

It is time to reflect on how perceptions are shaped by attitudes and beliefs, ultimately impacting our reality and causing spiritual confinement. Instead of blindly following traditions, we should recognize the power of critical thinking and the importance of trust in building a better society. Beliefs, when not grounded in understanding and reason, can indeed become a source of vulnerability.

Let us move towards embracing our own potential and purpose, rather than worshiping and praying to figures that might hinder our progress. It is essential to question and challenge outdated

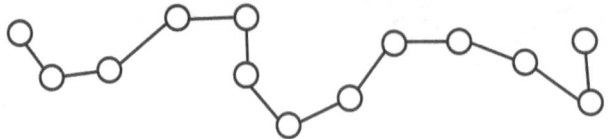

ideologies that no longer serve our collective well-being. By doing so, we can aspire to create a more enlightened and compassionate world.

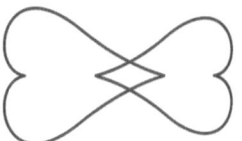 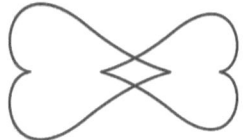

Deception Through Altered Reality

Ultimately, the perception of reality is greatly influenced by the prevailing societal norms and narratives. In a society that upholds the principles of free will and free speech, those who challenge the status quo or question the established reality are often perceived as vulnerable targets, while those who assert themselves aggressively may be seen as imposing spiritual dominance.

The concept of equality among all human beings raises important questions. Regardless of religious beliefs such as Christianity's assertion of immaculate conception, we are fundamentally created in the same manner, and this common origin should be acknowledged. It is crucial to critically examine claims that appear to be aimed at consolidating control over individuals, similar to what might be seen in the strategies employed by criminal syndicates. Fear, shame, and guilt can be tools utilized by such groups to maintain power over their followers, raising concerns about the potential cult-like nature of such practices.

In an alternate perspective, the terms "religion" and "cult" can be viewed as having similar connotations, referring to systems where those in authority administer beliefs and followers adhere

to established historical doctrines that have often concentrated power among the wealthy and historically dominant.

The intoxicating allure of power can lead those in authority to fear losing their control, perpetuating a system where the common people may be relegated to a subservient role. The notion of the "American dream" takes on a different light when considering the significant loss of human lives, around 60 million, due to historical events driven by a desire for wealth and dominance. The control of historical narratives by the conquering parties can justify their actions through deception, influencing the outcomes in their favor.

By manipulating perception, certain entities attempt to reshape reality, concealing undesirable aspects akin to sweeping crumbs under a rug—out of sight and out of mind. It may seem amusing to attribute responsibility for death and destruction to Santa, metaphorically highlighting how deceptive tactics can obscure the truth.

Allowing traditions and societal norms to be influenced by deception and organizations can perpetuate a cycle of history repeating itself. The question arises: why have we, as a society, remained ignorant for so many millennia? Perhaps this ignorance has served the purpose of

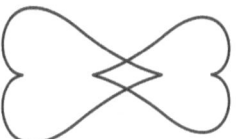 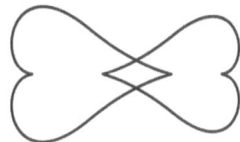

suppressing human spirit and diverting us from understanding our true purpose in the present.

To effect meaningful change, it becomes essential to confront and address the corruption that permeates various levels of society. Only by bringing these issues to light, analyzing them thoroughly, and making necessary corrections can we pave the way for genuine transformation.

Human history is marked by past wrongdoings against our fellow beings, and across various cultures, flood legends symbolize the idea of a fresh start or cleansing. These memories represent only a recent portion of an extensive and infinite account, which creationism may help us comprehend. Considering the vastness of the universe, assuming that we are the most intelligent life would be limiting and narrow-minded, potentially hindering our progress. The true understanding of wellness and wholeness goes beyond this perspective and transcends dualism.

Throughout history, deception has been used to manipulate perception, leading to ongoing battles for dominance. It is crucial to be cautious about where we place our trust, as many seek to influence others without fully understanding themselves. Our human race often seems uncertain about its true nature, relying on labels and group opinions to define everything, leaving

individuality overlooked. Reconnecting with personal intuition, which might have been more prevalent in ancient civilizations, can be a way to rediscover our authentic selves and foster a deeper understanding of our place in the world.

There are ancient civilizations that predate mainstream historical records, and the true nature of a soul's journey, encompassing experiences on this planet or beyond, remains a profound mystery, captivating the minds of mystics throughout history. Defining the essence of the soul proves incredibly challenging and elusive.

The art of healing involves transforming pain and suffering into abundance and joy, serving as a personal goal for individuals. A commitment to happiness, health, balance, and wisdom becomes essential. It is crucial not to succumb to negativity or use it as an excuse to allow adverse circumstances to ruin one's life. Knowing when to walk away from such situations and looking forward rather than dwelling on the past becomes paramount. Success, in this context, can be measured by one's dedication to personal growth and the positive contributions made to others.

In a society that may seem troubled, conventional achievements are often tied to material possessions, social status, financial wealth, political affiliations, religious aspirations, and

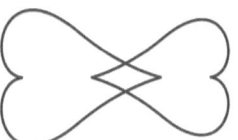 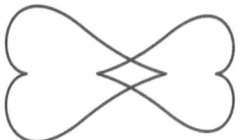

acquired professions. However, these symbols of status merely represent projections of wealth and temporal comfort. True aspirations should revolve around attaining independence, sovereignty, free thought, and a sense of well-being. Gratitude for the opportunity to live, love, and learn should be at the core of our existence. As long as society continues to value success based on superficial standards, humanity risks losing touch with the genuine purpose of the soul.

Critical change will be needed in perception of our goings on our interconnectedness to all life and creations. When our own inner beauty can shine our outer world will reflect all things in their natural state. What we were created to be not what projections have misled us to be. So, the people who were indigenous are wiped out. So, colonialism can overtake the land, bring in slaves and make the land profitable.

The level to which slavery and it over all impact on the specie of us all truly is the dark side of who and what we are. Slave breeding in the Americas, after the African coast pipeline was closed off. Sickened entitled land master`s forcing women to increase population.

In my estimation the very race we come from has always been a product of slavery. Even in the current system we have not been able to break free of an economic system that beholden us to a

9 to 5 mortgage necessities like food, cloths and other essential needs that make up the fabric of an experimental project that is so completely out of balance no wonder it`s my first impression that this planet has gone insane. A critical shift in perception is essential to recognize our interconnectedness with all life and creations. When we embrace our inner beauty and authenticity, the external world will naturally reflect harmony in its true state—the way we were meant to be, free from misleading projections.

The dark history of wiping out indigenous peoples and exploiting colonialism to make lands profitable, often through the use of slavery, is a painful reminder of the darker aspects of human history. Slave breeding in the Americas, particularly after the closure of the African coast pipeline, is a disturbing testament to the inhumane impact on the entire human species.

Throughout history, our race has, to a great extent, been shaped by the legacy of slavery. Even in our current economic system, we find ourselves bound by mortgages and basic necessities like food and clothing, all of which create an imbalanced reality. It is no wonder that one might perceive the state of our planet as a reflection of collective insanity.

Achieving a more sustainable and balanced existence will require a profound reevaluation of

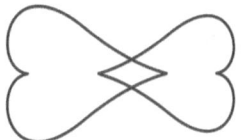 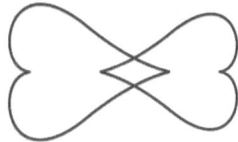

our values and a shift away from systems that perpetuate inequality and exploitation. Only by embracing empathy, compassion, and a deeper understanding of our interconnectedness can we hope to create a world that is truly harmonious and just for all.

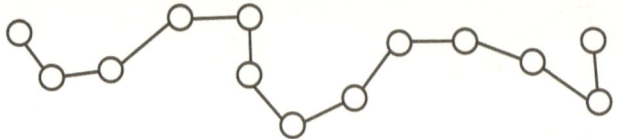

Perceptions Over Intuition

The blurring of our sense of purpose in the present is deeply influenced by societal norms and pressures. The problem lies in allowing external reality to dictate our beliefs and actions rather than embracing independent, free thought. Unfortunately, the significance of intuition and its role in leading a balanced life often goes overlooked in our society.

It seems that humanity's ability to engage in critical thinking and exercise true free will has been dulled over time, raising questions about the essential reasons for our existence. There is a prevalent focus on rational thought while neglecting the importance of emotional health, intuition, and heartfelt experiences. Living purely through an icy, detached approach does not seem to make sense when we should cherish and embrace our emotions and deep intuitive insights.

Perhaps leaders of faith fear a new collective awakening, where we come together as independent yet interconnected individuals, challenging the stagnant narrative of separation and division that has hindered our evolution. The fear of losing control, power, and authority could

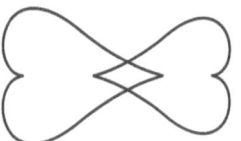 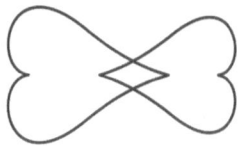

indeed be the driving force behind resistance to such a change.

The fuse for questioning authority's abuse of power was ignited through historical events involving colonialism, which resulted in the destruction of many cultures and their knowledge. This deeper understanding of our human experiment could lead to a more enlightened path, one that embraces our intuition and emotional wisdom to foster genuine progress and unity.

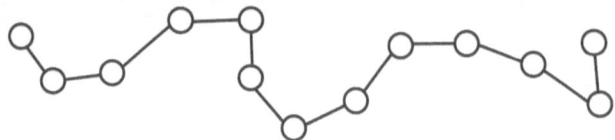

**A silent mind is a content heart
Only through an inspired heart is
Greatness achievable.**

 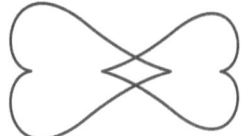

It is essential to trust our intuition and avoid allowing emotionally harmful perceptions to take root in our thoughts. When negativity prevails, it leads to collective losses for all of us. Those who project negativity or false beliefs, even if they claim justification, have a detrimental impact on our species. This manipulation has created significant gaps in what might have otherwise been a conceptually perfect world.

The dualistic approach of pursuing a greater good through widespread empire-building has come at the expense of the rights and freedoms of others. An ethical path to independence should never be influenced by religious justification, as it often results in the abuse of power. Such sick and abusive authority seeks to exert dominion over people's lives, perpetuating a cycle of oppression and harm. To foster genuine progress and harmony, we must uphold ethical principles that respect the rights and autonomy of all individuals.

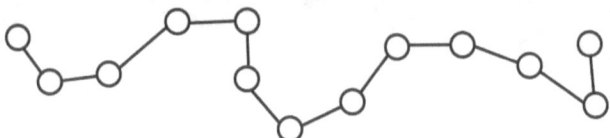

Personal notes:

In the name of Salvation:

Conform or die. Listen don't speak. Bow to maker as we have told.

The strong must rise to preserve evolution and growth

When conformity has run its course

Devised to divide what we hide

Creation is seen through the eyes of nature

When it's time to walk away don't look back

Our only fear should be that we never figured out who and what we are

Contentment is sound through soul purpose, free will and unconditional love allows an unimposing system by which healthy growth is individually achieved

Tyrannies tears are the blood of its subjects

Thoughts create reality

Emotions create situations

Situations are built on criteria

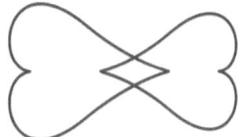 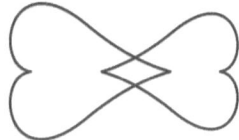

Resolutions are accomplished through compromise

So, what have we compromised due to the current form of authority

True power and freedom!!

Govern and corrected; lifted, gifted, guided and protected

The sick and sad reality of religion:

The alarming reality of some institutions is their control and manipulation over the spirits and souls of their followers, often treating them like sheep, conforming, conditioning, and brainwashing them. This manipulation is a tragic calamity for humanity, orchestrated through scriptures aimed at maintaining control and power. Unfortunately, the future appears bleak for those who abuse their power and those who follow such harmful ideologies.

Discrimination will no longer be shielded or overlooked, as false narratives and symbols, regardless of their significance, will be exposed under the piercing light of truth. The cross, star, or any other symbols that once offered refuge will not hide the dark realities behind them any longer. The time has come for transparency and accountability, ensuring that abusive practices are no longer tolerated.

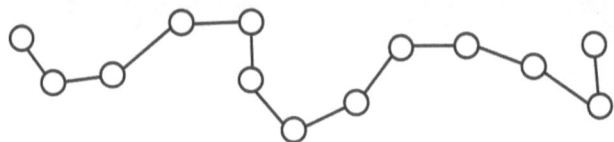

Conquest of Colonization

Goal

Conformity

Technique

Assert Power

Result

Dominance

By Product

Slavery

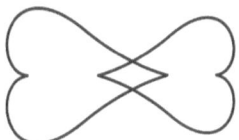 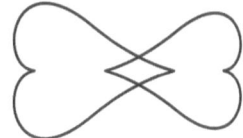

What power fears:

As sovereign beings, we must reclaim the power that was rightfully ours from birth. The power struggles and separations that have plagued this planet will eventually fade away with the institutions that propagated them. Empires may rise and fall, but the unwavering trust in our hearts remains constant. Unconditional love serves as the most potent remedy for the soul, nurturing a space where we can truly thrive.

It is time for humanity to unite and expose any nefarious intentions that have harmed us and our planet. Acknowledging the Earth as a living, breathing organism with its own spirit, following its unique timeline, empowers us to cherish and honor this sacred connection. Our love for the Earth enables us to explore, learn, and grow in the directions we choose, free to manifest our dreams and glorify our existence.

Whether it was God who created us or men who crafted the concept of God, there is no denying that our very experience is sustained by this Earth. Our stewardship of her should be the central focus of any narrative. What benefits the Earth's well-being also contributes to our own health and prosperity. Cultivating gratitude on a consistent basis can significantly improve life on this celestial rock hurtling through space.

In making future decisions, my priority is to consider what is genuinely right for me. Loyalty to the value of relationships matters greatly, focusing not on what I stand to gain, but on what I should avoid. I remain steadfast in not compromising my core values or seeking to appease others. When the time comes to move on, I aim to do so gracefully, without causing chaos or unnecessary disruption.

Conflict:

Strong opinions have the potential to ignite conflict, and thus, it is crucial to be mindful of their impact. The word "love" is frequently used as a tool of manipulation, so it's essential to pay attention to genuine emotions rather than just relying on verbal expressions.

The significance of this to me lies in the understanding that love should be reciprocated and healthy. If the love I give is not returned, it becomes one-sided and potentially detrimental. In truth, actions speak louder than words, and love should be demonstrated through genuine gestures and behavior. Remaining attached to ignorance or bliss can hinder growth, as it suggests complacency and a reluctance to progress. It is essential to avoid becoming stagnant and instead strive for continuous improvement rather than resting on one's laurels.

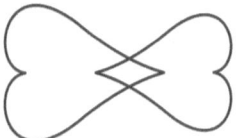 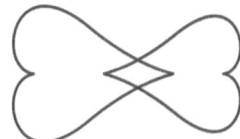

Personal notes:

The enemy lives within each of us, and so do the answers.

Within creation without distractions.

When love leads the way human kind will see real freedom.

Darkness is illuminated with compassion.

True compassions has no strings attached, no false expectations and is not done for financial gain.

Through the tears dreams are made.

A weighted trigger has a predictable outcome.

Purpose of conformity: Power obligation of power: Stay in power.

Power obligation stay in power.

When seeking happiness from those around us, our best approach often involves being a positive influence. Occasionally, the path to contentment requires releasing attachments that hold deep significance. While this process may induce discomfort, its lessons prove invaluable. Our well-being and inner tranquility mustn't hinge upon the decisions of others, even if their choices lead to adversity for the vulnerable.

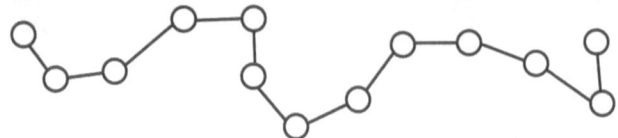

Throughout history, the archetype of the "bully" has persisted. Intriguingly, it's arguable that the bully's responses mirror those who opt for compassion and affection over dominance and authority. The dynamic between opposing energies is a compelling facet of human existence. Acknowledging that we're not at fault for the addictive allure of these polarities, it's crucial to recognize that overindulgence in either direction can yield dire consequences.

The elusive equilibrium between these forces poses a perplexing quandary. Yet, the solution is remarkably uncomplicated: the practice of unconditional love, harmonized with well-defined boundaries rooted in trust, respect, and transparency. Among these virtues, honesty emerges as paramount. Its capacity to dismantle artifice and engender humility is profound, fostering the germination of transformative seeds.

A pivotal stride in our journey involves conceding our fallibility, particularly when confronted with untenable circumstances. The ability to admit misconceptions and adapt marks a trajectory toward rectification. Forsaking our own potential precipitates despondency, underscoring the necessity of nurturing self-belief.

Striking a balance in our aspirations is pivotal; an abundance of hope, though inspiring, can yield precarious disproportion. Like other fundamental

 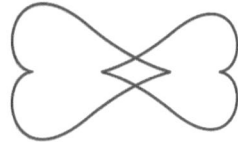

emotions, excessive hope lacks rationality and equilibrium. To reorient ourselves, it's imperative to recalibrate our relationship with optimism.

Consider the intriguing notion that each emotional current resonates with a distinct frequency, creating a unique imprint within the universe. When our essence resonates with love, the cosmos bestows its rewards, a phenomenon that echoes the principles of the law of attraction.

In essence, your exploration delves into the intricate tapestry of human emotions, relationships, and personal evolution. It underlines the importance of self-awareness, the art of balance, and the enduring power of genuine, unadulterated love.

Our current reality resembles a complex scientific inquiry, where a multitude of genetic code sequences intricately shape the present moment. Regrettably, the genetic makeup inclined towards wielding power has largely dictated the fabric of society. However, as individuals whose genetic predisposition favors creativity and growth ascend, a harmonious equilibrium is poised to grace our planet. Picture the celestial sphere that houses this reality—a planet suspended in space—poised for transformation as novel concepts emerge.

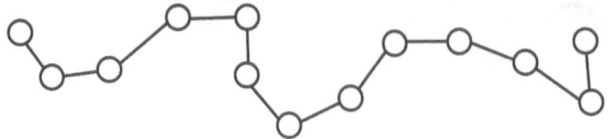

The genesis of groundbreaking ideas often occurs beyond the confines of convention, a realm power seeks to control. It's a vital truth that power is primarily preoccupied with safeguarding its dominion. The allure of temptation exerts its pull, stirring the debate of whether the cup is half full or half empty. But a cup brimming with abundance gazes beyond the lures of temptation.

In this narrative, the current state of affairs takes on the aura of an intricate experiment, orchestrated by the interplay of genetic codes. Those genetically inclined towards authority have, unfortunately, exerted a dominant influence on society. However, as individuals bearing codes primed for innovation and progress ascend, a symphonic equilibrium awaits our planet. Imagine, if you will, our world—a celestial orb adrift in the cosmos—on the cusp of a transformative dawn as radical concepts germinate.

The genesis of pioneering notions often unfolds beyond the constraints of conformity, a domain that power relentlessly seeks to harness. A pivotal understanding surfaces: power's preeminent concern revolves around preserving its ascendancy. The allure of temptation tugs at us, igniting the age-old debate of whether the cup stands half full or half empty. Yet, within a vessel brimming with plenitude, the allure of temptation wanes.

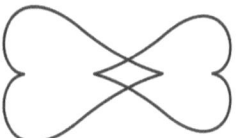 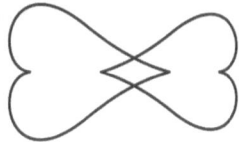

Your perspective casts our reality as a profound scientific exploration, where genetic sequences interweave to define the present. It underscores the influence of power, contrasts it against the promise of creative emergence, and illuminates the interplay between temptation and abundance.

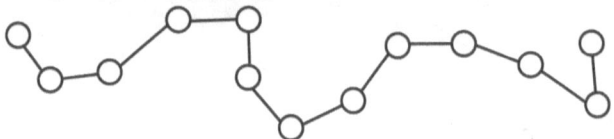

Personal notes:

Charming adorable instead of sexy.

Conformity is slavery in decease.

Ignorance feeds a future that has no concept.

The future is shaped by what is created today.

Conformity has a predictable future.

Conformity feeding evil. Evil feeding control. Control staying in power ignorance.

Do you define the world around you or does it define you?

Never have I encountered a soul like yours. After touching it I don't have the correct words to describe your true essence properly.

A master is not afraid to be a student.

Respect earned is a respect given.

If the tears are the price we pay

They become priceless.

When we see endings as new beginnings we have grown and learned.

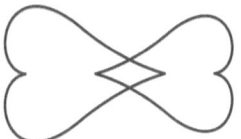 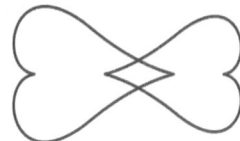

Awake but not fully aware.

Identify personality traits that speak to the heart space.

Tornado image rebuild.

Spiritual reunion on a soul level, nothing physical.

Make sure can't go back commitment, devotion, dedication, love, heart energy.

The dark soul wants what it wants.

Just like the light soul wants what it wants.

Dark soul destructive behavior like conformity.

Light soul share courage, hope, strength and unconditional love.

Deserving hearts suffer while undeserving hearts abuse and control.

Trauma bond or loving bond.

The manner in which we express our boundless love serves as a mirror reflecting our self-love. An inherent human vulnerability has, unfortunately, been exploited by organized religious institutions under the guise of love. This manipulation begets a disturbing cycle—where fear is used as a tool and salvation is contorted into a form of affliction. It is amidst this milieu that genuine spirituality stands as a formidable adversary to organized

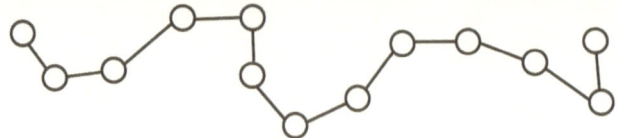

religion, unafraid to recognize darkness for what it is.

True visionaries, unburdened by the need for followers, instead empower others to step into leadership roles. Yet, as the earth's surface seems to deflate under the weight of exploitation, a crucial question arises: Can mere deflation suffice? Urgency beckons for intervention as concealed knowledge languishes, ensnared by the tentacles of corporate power—a power keen on preserving its dominion over us, the unwitting pawns. Conformity remains its reigning instrument.

Amidst this intricate web, the future finds its genesis in the present moment. The very fabric of human goodness erodes when silence shrouds virtuous deeds. To rekindle the flickering soul of humanity, the resounding call of one's authentic inner voice must be heeded—a voice borne of profound wisdom that necessitates action.

A transformative juncture awaits: a juncture wherein collective intentions coalesce to nurture the entirety of our planet. Humanity's evolution hinges upon this collective shift. Yet, as the battle for control rages on, surrendering to power allows its triumph. Stepping beyond self, brave souls engage in acts of altruism—bold acts that demand unyielding courage.

 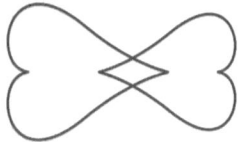

In the quest for authenticity, voices once stifled emerge resoundingly, attesting to the resurgence of individual empowerment. The epoch has dawned for power-driven institutions to relinquish their arms and cede to a more enlightened ethos. As the prevailing hive mind, a conglomerate of thoughts, wanes, a promising harbinger of positive change emerges—a beacon guiding humanity towards a brighter collective consciousness.

Your insight delves into the complex dynamics of love, manipulation, spirituality, and empowerment. It underscores the pivotal role of individual action in shaping a harmonious world, while also illuminating the potential for a transformative shift in societal paradigms.

Twisted lies vs. truth verses

Negative messaging to positive influence

Commandments /rules freewill

Sad when the only person we can trust is our self.

Agnostic- undecided

Atheist- denial

Religion-corrupt-false ego- narcissist

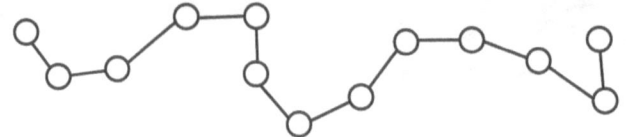

Spirituality can be distilled to a profound recognition of creation unfolding in each moment, an intimate connection we share as conscious participants. This journey involves a deep-rooted love for ourselves and the Earth, extending towards fellow human beings whose resonance aligns harmoniously with our own. These are individuals who authentically inhabit their truth, transcending labels to embrace a pure and unadulterated spiritual essence.

What moved by the men made holy spirit means from my prospective:

The essence of a person's soul has been subdued and pilfered, transforming their physical vessel into a mere tool of rigid religious conformity, entwined with the tumultuous ebbs and flows of emotional turbulence. The inexorable laws of cause and effect cast their shadow over history's cyclical repetition, a testament to the prolonged slumber humanity has endured under the sway of influences unknown for an unfathomable span. A singular truth, distinctly personal, eludes imposition and must be unearthed, not imposed through the distorted lens of misinterpreted historical narratives.

Once vibrant energy conduits encircling our planet have fallen victim to the malevolent designs of cowardly purveyors of religious dogma.

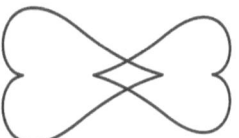 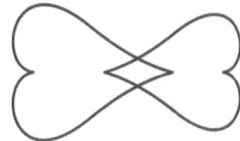

While the prospect of restoration resides within these sanctuaries of the profaned, their purpose transcends their usurpation by any creed or doctrine. The very vibrational cadence, the OMH, holds the key to healing, disentangled from the fervent beliefs of men, gods, or ethereal spirits. Our path to rejuvenation lies in our bond with the Earth Mother and our unwavering reverence for her, unfurling as the conduit for our healing.

An ardent gratitude for every fleeting moment gifted to us in the tapestry of existence weaves a profound connection with our creation. The solemn adieu to the callous dominion of religious dogma, though born from a tumultuous past, charts a trajectory where humanity embraces symbiosis with the Earth Mother and all her inhabitants.

The enigma of why this calamity has befallen us remains veiled, shrouded in ambiguity. Perhaps it serves as the crucible through which we rekindle our intrinsic uniqueness, enabling us to partake in the cosmic narrative of an ever-expanding universe. This epoch bares a significance, profound yet elusive, in our ceaseless evolution, a chapter of our journey whose implications remain tantalizingly beyond reach.

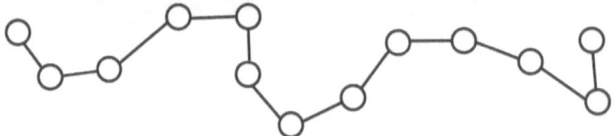

Personal notes:

What's worth wailing for shouldn't need to be fought for

Cults need a leader regardless the lamb sacrificed in order to carry out its destruction in this here and now.

An angry hater is in defense of their cult mentality

Destroy what is not understood.

Resolve?

Fight it with peace and love and let it fracture itself

Wait, watch, laugh.

Limiting the origin and culmination of creation solely to Earth and its denizens reflects a narrow perspective on the vast expanse of the universe. Embracing the notion that human intelligence embodies a cosmic encoding offers a more expansive and enlightened viewpoint, one that transcends the confines of our planet and encompasses the profound intricacies of soul and spirituality.

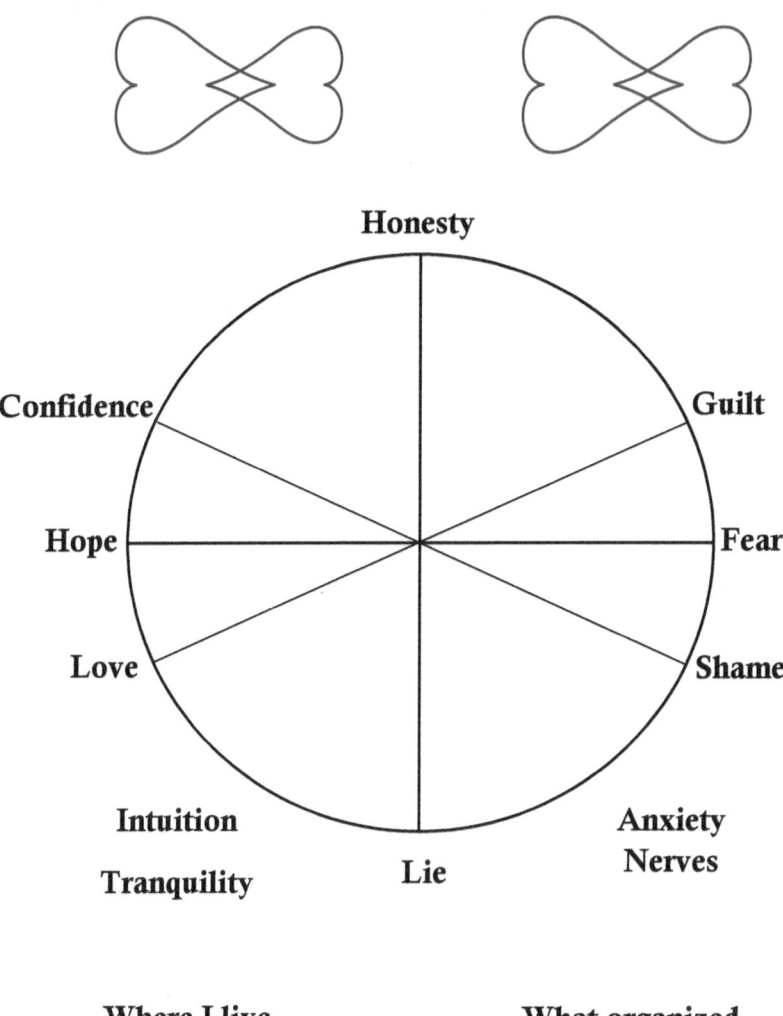

Traces of blood mar the ceiling, a grim testament to the violence that pervades. Humanity's self-inflicted wounds stain the very ground upon which it treads. The ceaseless cycle of conflict must relinquish its grip on our collective destiny, replaced by a resolute commitment to attentive understanding if we are to endure.

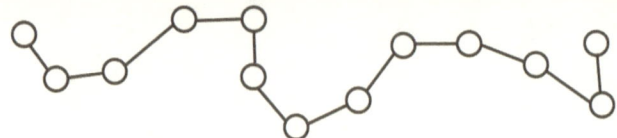

Words, once mere symbols, have become vessels laden with potent emotions, a human construct imbued with layers of significance. This intricate entwining of language and sentiment finds its roots in the labyrinth of human conditioning—a mechanism devised to exert influence. However, the reins of control can no longer dictate the narrative; a paradigm shift beckons, led by the unfettered minds of innovators. It is these visionary thinkers who hold the key to ushering in novel concepts, carving pathways to a profoundly fulfilling existence within this awe-inspiring realm.

Anticipate formidable resistance on this transformative journey. Within the grand tapestry of evolution, does my role hold sway? The intricate lattice of entrenched behaviors and inherited norms remains pivotal—a nexus where growth and struggle converge. Authenticity emerges as the cornerstone; it is through the reclamation of individual truths that we forge our path as sovereign spiritual beings, a pivotal shift that promises to recalibrate the world. With collective intent, may our aspirations burgeon, each crafting their unique tapestry of peace and love—a rightful birthright. Vigilance guards against relinquishing the reins to any collective entity; instead, let positive influence stand as the catalyst. Our hearts' emissaries, we sow the seeds of change, envisioning a realm free from discord

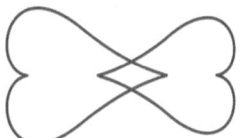 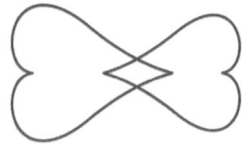

and conflict, a harmonious existence conjured from the depths of imagination.

Envision a world adorned with tranquil resolutions, a realm free from the grip of power-hungry dominion. Should we embrace non-judgmental empathy, extending compassion not only to our neighbors but to all who traverse our shared paths, a pivotal juncture awaits. The very fabric of this planet reverberates with heightened energy, an undeniable force that beckons humanity to shape its narrative. The choices woven into this vibrant tapestry will undoubtedly etch our historical legacy. May we reclaim our rightful place within the cosmic order, an aspiration that holds the potential to redefine our trajectory.

Consider this scenario: if I were to share my enthusiasm for a new shampoo I've discovered, would you be inclined to give it a try? In a similar vein, suppose I introduced you to a transformative way of harmonizing our existence with the world around us, potentially prompting a shift away from traditional religious affiliations in favor of embracing open-minded expression. Unplugging from the societal currents saturated with negativity reveals a realm where boundless possibilities unfurl. Society's sustenance seemingly stems from human suffering, stress, anxiety, and a prevailing sense of despair—an environment that fosters the illusion of success

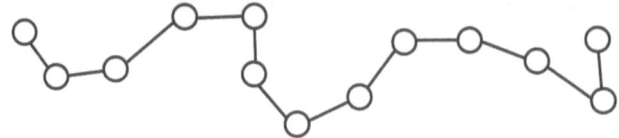

as an addictive pursuit, perpetuating a self-centric, ego-driven yearning for validation. Yet, this battle can be triumphed through the profound wisdom of the heart. However, the question lingers: does embodying a positive influence alone suffice as a soul's purpose? The answer, perhaps, is a resounding no.

Spiritual crisis-You are the canoe. Life is the river (past), stream(present) or pond (now).

If you don`t get ready for life you will be swept down river, the stream and pond are upriver.

Desperation, often associated with bipolar disorder, manifests as an overwhelming sense of hopelessness where all facets of life seem to unravel. A pervasive feeling of entrapment emerges, eroding one's individuality, sapping confidence, and distorting self-perception. This tumultuous state can lead to a psychic fracture, as if the very world is imploding, potentially even evoking a sense of abandonment by a higher power. A possible remedy resides in a profound shift: owning one's behavior that precipitated this collapse, rejecting the role of victim that societal norms might impose. Liberating oneself from the clutches of victimhood, refraining from pharmaceutical interventions that lack conscience, and instead, harnessing the innate human capacity for positive change, offers a

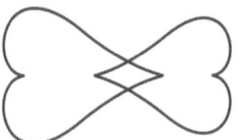 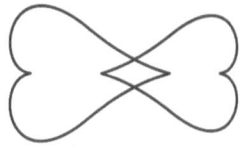

transformative path forward, inspiring a life of resilience and well-being.

The profound awareness that dawns with each breath underscores the preciousness of life itself. The relentless spiral of negativity is yielding to a transformation, spurred by awakening one individual at a time. Embracing the role of an open vessel, we beseech to be imbued with love, light, hope, wisdom, and guidance. The shackles of institutionalized religion, once wielded for control, find redemption through humanity's aspiration for genuine and unencumbered self-expression. The cosmos witnesses with understanding as forgiveness unfurls for those who unknowingly inflicted harm. Let the cynics voice their dissent; beneath their animosity lies a void that love, true and unwavering, has the power to fill. Beneath their veneer of hatred, they grapple with a self-loathing they dare not confront, yet an authentic love possesses the potential to dissolve such darkness. Your essence is now pure, and you possess the divine right to reshape this world to align with its intended purpose. As destiny's gentle knock ushers change, be open to its gradual entrance. I shall serve as your guide, a singular beacon amidst a myriad of earthly manifestations that pale in significance. You, yourself, elected this journey; your soul's mission is your own doing. The exalted divine purpose, while fraught with risks, finds you unswervingly prepared. The sanctity of

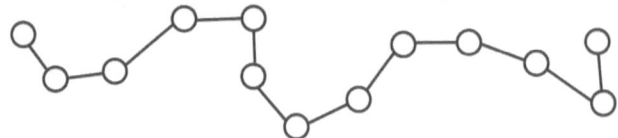

each breath must either prevail consistently or relinquish its sanctity entirely; no compromise can suffice. The ephemeral veneer of righteousness sustained merely on Sundays is a disservice to the profound depth of your being.

In the delicate balance between spiritual liberation and material entrapment, the choice is ours to make. The spectrum spans from emotional equilibrium to a turbulent rollercoaster of feelings, from open-minded exploration to the confines of a closed perspective. At the crossroads of embracing change and retreating to the comfort of the familiar lies a pivotal decision—will we be guided by wisdom or hindered by ignorance? Consider, if I were to share a discovery—an intrinsic treasure untainted by the influence of organized institutions—what would your response be? Would you deem it implausible? Reflect, for it is when the heart finds contentment in simplicity that it blossoms into a vessel of gratitude and grace, a disposition that remains unaltered by the fluctuations of abundance or scarcity.

When possessions define us, our character becomes flawed - Philanthropy

My endeavor to articulate the ineffable essence of words that elude precise expression centers around an innate knowing—an intuitive

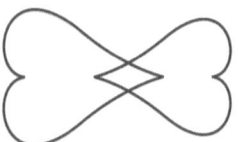 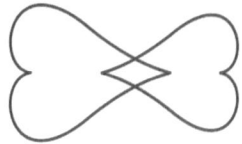

awareness that, through the prism of positivity, destiny's design shall seamlessly intersect with my path. However, it is vital to avoid complacency, for reclining upon one's laurels will not suffice in ushering forth the grandeur of envisioned aspirations. Rather, it is our unyielding faith in these dreams that distinguishes us from societal conventions, propelling us towards unparalleled realms of achievement that transcend earthly metrics.

Much akin to the boundless expanse of the cosmos, bereft of a discernible origin or termination, the potential of our triumphs defies quantification upon this terrestrial plane. This analogy echoes a sentiment often disregarded by both the rigid constraints of scientific analysis and the dogmatic tenets of organized religion. It is within the realm of metaphysics that the veils are lifted, and an experiential tapestry unfurls. Metaphysics, in its essence, is an immersive voyage, not a mere dictum or empirical endeavor.

The enigma that resides within each individual's soul defies rational explication or logical justification. This enigma, however, encapsulates the sublime beauty of human existence, encapsulated within the vessel of our corporeal forms. Every individual embarks upon a purposeful odyssey, a journey intrinsically linked to the cosmic symphony—a tapestry of information perpetually cascading like ethereal

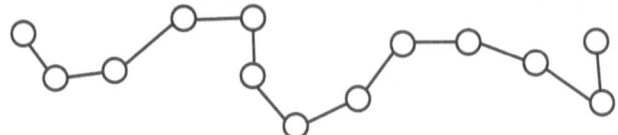

stardust. Skepticism may raise its voice, but such skepticism is a reflection of its own nature. Meanwhile, I stand serenely amidst a tranquil aura, brimming with love and inspiration, poised to ardently fulfill the destiny that resonates within the depths of my soul.

Salvation: the quintessential elixir of alchemists, a transcendental panacea that elicits an intoxicating euphoria, devoid of conventional intoxication. The alchemist's miscalculation lay in underestimating the potency of authentic, unwavering love—a love that empowers all souls to realize their latent potential, unfurling purpose with an innate candor, unveiling the buried verities within.

At its core, the crux of the matter revolves around the predilection of men to wield dominion over their compatriots. It is a pursuit that inadvertently blinds them to the profound virtues of equanimity, where souls thrive in unison, each pursuing their path without the imposition of doctrinal sermons. Amidst this enigma, emerges a vanguard of awakened spirits—myself included—bearing a profound verity, destined to rectify the prevailing disarray. Our mission: to harmonize this enigmatic realm, to resurrect its magical equilibrium. An appellation reminiscent of Eden may be bestowed, a paradisiacal haven where the flock, unfortunately, grazes upon the bitter herbage of negativity.

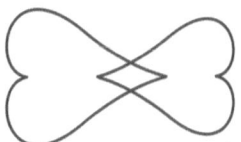 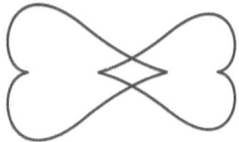

Personally, I stand emancipated from the notion of personal salvation. Rather, it is the inhabitants who beckon for deliverance from the mire of their own discord. The malaise of pessimism, the constricting tendrils of negativity, necessitate purification, thereby unveiling the inherent luminescence of our essence—a luminosity radiating as a celestial beacon within the vast cosmos. This is not an edict, not a doctrine to adhere to; it is our innate birthright, an unwavering trust in the cosmos, untethered by the chains of conformity.

In the realm of open-minded free thinkers, the coexistence within our present reality exacts a considerable toll on the human psyche. The burdensome weight of this earthly plane often clashes with an alternative dimension brimming with profound thought, expansive knowledge, and sagacious wisdom—an ethereal realm eager to infuse our immediate existence with newfound insights. Yet, frustratingly, the fabric of our immediate reality repels these offerings, leaving us grappling to convey the richness of our unique perspectives. This struggle lies in our inability to fully articulate the extraordinary gifts we bare, gifts that elevate us to ever-greater tiers of consciousness.

In our collective desire, none among us yearns to awaken from one nightmare only to be ensnared in the clutches of another. The quest for

unattainable perfection often becomes a self-defeating endeavor, fraught with perilous risks, some of which may prove fatal. Nevertheless, avenues to serenity unfurl before us: through meditation, embracing a wholesome diet, engaging in invigorating exercise, and cultivating a profound self-love, we ascend thresholds that elevate our awareness.

The travesty of a conventional education, which regrettably leaves the human spirit overweight with ignorance, is undeniable. The ardent pursuit of financial success, in the face of such consequences, stands bereft of true worth. Gratitude must be extended to societal norms, albeit begrudgingly, for illuminating the conspicuous flaws in this paradigm.

In the realm of virtues and morals, we confront our most profound quandary. These twin pillars of humanity's essence remain elusive in their measurement. It is within this very crucible that the concept of "good" finds its genesis. What perplexes is the audacity of organized religion to claim credit for these quintessential human interactions, intrinsic to our character. Even when marred by imperfections, the justification often arises—a weak premise indeed. Unconditional love, however, requires no such validation; it resides within the sanctum of heart and soul, a beacon guiding our path.

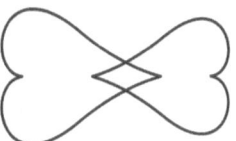 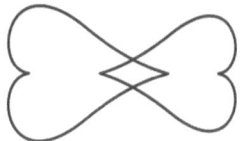

Upon scrutinizing organized religion and its effects on the individual, a troubling pattern emerges: one of obligation born from fear or shame. Virtues and morals, in truth, are experiential entities, their teachings grounded in the rich soil of unconditional love. Commencement of this journey starts with self-love, and herein lies the disquieting flaw within the hierarchical structure of organized religion. Its rectification necessitates a renaissance, a shedding of dominion over humanity, and a rebirth founded upon purity. In this rejuvenated paradigm, the emblem of "good" would persist as a symbol of love and guidance, transcending the vulgar visage of a human form crucified.

Embarking on a journey of emotional restoration, the process of healing is intricately woven with the fabric of our feelings. As we consciously divert our attention away from the shadows of negativity that once dominated our thoughts, a profound transformation occurs: the doors of our minds swing shut on these adverse influences, granting passage to an influx of positivity. The human experience, a reservoir of accumulated adversities from myriad soul cycles, may appear as an imposing mountain, its summit seemingly insurmountable. Yet, a shift in focus becomes paramount, a redirection toward the wisdom distilled from life's lessons and an unwavering understanding of our intrinsic purpose.

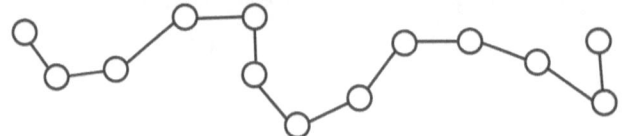

Although the concept of salvation casts a faint shadow upon this narrative, it is a nuanced reflection. Rather, the crux of the matter lies in our ownership of behavior and the cultivation of a pristine conscience. This dual mastery not only kindles a profound metamorphosis within our own lives but also ignites the radiant beacon of influence, inspiring others to tread a similar path. Our self-assuredness reverberates, a symphony of empowerment that elicits two distinct reactions from the world: an awe-inspired attraction or a veiled intimidation.

In this symphony of transformation, the underestimation of envy must be avoided—a potent force that arises when those overshadowed by their own limitations encounter the luminance of positive goodness. To wield such insight is to navigate the delicate intricacies of human interaction with sagacity and grace, ushering forth a harmonious melody that resonates not only within us but also throughout the tapestry of existence.

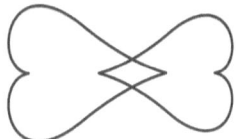 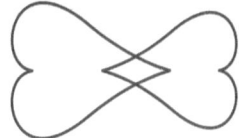

Personal notes:

Who are you? A free and govern citizen of the cosmos.

Love's purpose is to be shared.

Fears purpose is to frighten.

Guilts purpose is to shame.

Shame's purpose is to control.

F*****g sick S**t!!!

Rising awareness:

Fundamentally, the prevailing reality remains that the pervasive tendrils of negative conditioning, cast upon humanity by society's hand, stand as formidable barriers to the attainment of heightened awareness. A corollary truth emerges: the immutable law of attraction. With unwavering vigilance, the cultivation of affirmative thoughts, the embodiment of respectful conduct, and a conscientious regard for one's physical vessel converge to elevate consciousness. Within this paradigm, the unassailable birthright of every soul emerges—a birthright that entitles each to ascend towards their zenith of potential, basking in the abundant shower of love's embrace.

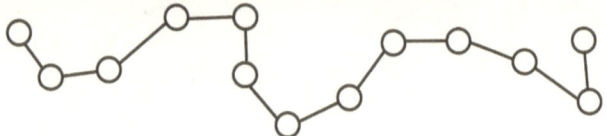

Personal notes:

Sweeter nectar attracts more love.

Lip service leads no where.

Action requires commitment.

Life of a sloth. Death of a pig.

Genuine, enduring love finds its roots in a profound self-cherishing that transcends any allure of material possessions or external gifts. To be ahead of the curve, rather than a step behind, is a lesson well learned. Acts of spontaneous kindness unfurl as emissaries of compassion, casting their benevolent ripples across the boundless expanse of the cosmos. The true essence of compassion, unblemished by ulterior motives, necessitates no spotlight for validation. A sentiment both mystifying and whimsical lies within the orchestration of existence, leaving the task of deciphering life's purpose to the individual—an irony not lost on the universe's cosmic jest.

While laced with a touch of sardonic humor, this cosmic design extends an invitation to reckon with our insecurities, those whispering shadows that cast a pall of fear. Reconciliation with these elements becomes the path to equilibrium.

 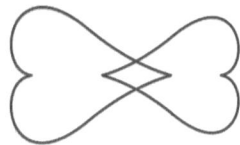

Determinedly, I shall navigate towards my destined purpose, a journey that could benefit from a surge of serendipitous synchronicity to smoothen the way, for the cosmos knows the cadence of the cosmic dance.

Salvation, a potent elixir surpassing the influence of any drug, emerges as a force of transformative might. However, the strategy of ensnaring and perpetuating dependency unveils a vulnerability in its design. The imposition of dogmatic directives, dictating the very fabric of existence, reveals a contrived and manipulative endeavor— a manifestation of past failures that have left humanity disillusioned across myriad dimensions. This overreach of authority has cast divisive shadows, estranging those of us who recognize the falsehood.

In contrast, the essence of divinity resides not within victimhood but flourishes within the fertile grounds of courage, resilience, unwavering commitment, boundless hope, boundless love, graciousness, indomitable determination, unrestrained freedom, unadulterated purity, and, paramount of all, an unwavering trust in the cosmic orchestrations—far removed from the pages of history, residing within the cosmic tapestry that threads through the universe.

Patterns of conduct and convictions that foster emotional dependency possess a potent capacity for detriment, notwithstanding their original benevolent motives. The mechanism of rationalization often extends a formidable lifeline to bolster its own existence. Amidst this intricate web of human tendencies, the psyche has undergone a gradual fragility, partly a consequence of the proliferation of modern comforts—ostensibly designed to streamline existence, yet paradoxically serving as conduits for bewilderment, disorder, and the unsettling undercurrent of anxiety, thus precipitating a disheartening descent of the human state.

In this complex milieu, the notion emerges: Is not life's tapestry mine to weave, my legacy to forge? The paradox intensifies when one contemplates the surrender of personal agency to external proclamations of inadequacy.

The notion that temptation's fruit leads to sin appears steeped in a kind of inverted ignorance—a narrative that curiously aligns with an organization's agenda, one that capitalizes on instilling fear and subsequently offers a remedy. This narrative wields formidable influence, tugging at the heartstrings of emotions, its potency undeniable. Amidst this intricate interplay, it becomes evident that only peace and love are essential, indispensable components for existence within this realm. One cannot help but

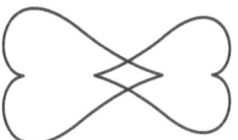 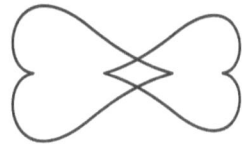

ponder the profusion of excuses, the profound layers of denial, and the willingness to relinquish personal sovereignty to conform to such an arrangement.

Is it mere ignorance at play, or do deeper currents surge beneath the surface? Could it be the deceptive yearning of souls to be embraced and validated? Perhaps comfort finds its abode in these notions, driven by an aversion to the discomfort of change. This intricate orchestration offers just enough sustenance to maintain the flock's allegiance, eliciting contributions of both time and finances in furtherance of its agenda. The allure of pseudo-contentment, attained through material accumulation, fosters a facade of happiness.

Yet, anchored in this stagnancy, no foundation can endure the relentless test of time. The crucial catalyst for transformation lies in the realm of change—change that invariably accompanies growth, albeit accompanied by the sting of discomfort. Can I, in truth, absorb the burdensome sorrows of others, offering them solace and disposing of their pain in a manner that is not detrimental to myself? The affirmative echoes resoundingly—a resounding commitment undertaken for the collective well-being. The world hungers for healers, those adept at bridging the chasm between the tangible and the ethereal, poised to unveil mysteries both known and veiled.

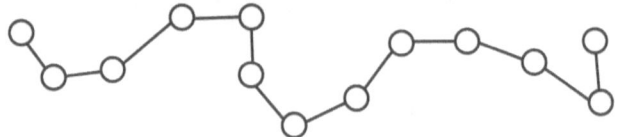

Gratitude envelops me for the wisdom amassed along this transformative odyssey, fostering an abiding reverence for the unfolding process.

Just when the cadence of learning appears to wane, a fresh challenge materializes, a testament to the inexorable growth that continues to unfold. My willingness to delve into the intricate tapestry of motivations and inquiries permits a measured ascent, ensuring sanity is retained. A heart brimming with love inherently demands expression and dissemination—a truth that reverberates through the very essence of existence.

An intriguing proposition arises:

Did ancient technologies possess the capacity for temporal travel? Could it be that we stand on the cusp of an impending juncture where all timelines converge and culminate? Perhaps this very concept sheds light on the sensation that permeates my days—moments when I seem to traverse diverse dimensions. Equally perplexing is the phenomenon of déjà vu—a sensation where the soul recognizes a precise location, though not within the confines of the present physical vessel.

String theory, a bedrock of modern physics, has unveiled the tantalizing realm of interdimensional existence. It is a realm that beckons

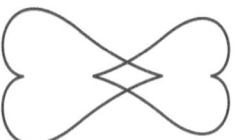 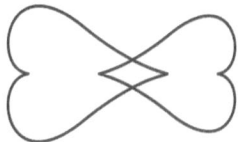

contemplation, prompting the question of whether my perceptions are mere whims of imagination or rather glimpses into these multifaceted realms. This musing carries an unexpected echo, reminiscent of states induced by psychedelic experiences.

Is there a realm of existence more profound than the enigmatic bond where two souls intertwine, birthing an unadulterated love that flourishes? Could this be akin to the transformative connection that takes root when a woman gives life to a child—the indelible tether binding mother and child? One ponders if humanity possesses the potential to foster such profound affection for one another, and if not, what catalyzes this divergence?

In contemplation, a shared origin emerges as the common thread woven through the tapestry of our existence. We all emanate from the same cosmic cradle, an undeniable unity inherently woven into our being. Yet, paradoxically, the fabric of humanity is marred by division, splintered by incongruences. While each individual radiates a unique essence, a common current pulse through our collective purpose—a purpose that seems to beckon us toward a singular destination: the embodiment and proliferation of love.

How is it that as a collective, we permit the insidious influence of pessimistic energies perpetuated through faith to shape our trajectory? It is an enigma, considering the remarkable strides we've made, juxtaposed against the emotional stagnation we seem to linger within. What is the underlying scheme, the intricate design that steers us down this bewildering path? Why do we endure this status quo, ensnared in its clutches? Is it that we are ensnared by distraction or swayed by deception, rendering us bereft of the fortitude to challenge the established order?

Amidst this labyrinth, a crucial query emerges: Does a divine purpose truly animate our existence? And curiously, why does it seem that whenever my soul makes its presence felt, the shadow of the Catholic Church metaphorically looms, akin to severing my sense of self?

The layers of these questions are profound, painting a portrait of our relentless pursuit of truth amidst the complex interplay of spiritual and societal paradigms.

In a calculated orchestration, deliberate polarization is employed, underpinned by concocted narratives, with both factions vying for supremacy. A power struggle ensues, wherein submission is inconceivable, and control begets control. Yet, the adversary of this regime of

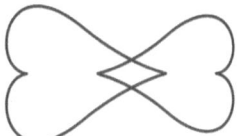 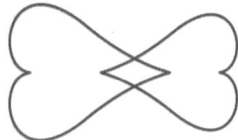

control is love coupled with comprehension. The strategic appeal to control through the conduit of love paves the way for those crucial dialogues essential for compromise and collective growth.

This civilization, akin to its predecessors that have graced this planetary canvas, will too wane. Its foundation rests upon the same bedrock of power dynamics that have underpinned myriad civilized societies before it. A beacon of promise emerges in the form of change—a transformative force that could potentially mold a new reality. Nostalgic recollections surface of inscribing timeless sentiments onto notes for a cherished partner, those words 'forever' bearing weight and significance beyond comprehension.

The trajectory of our evolution seems suspended, particularly in matters of spirituality and the vast potential it harbors. In the realm of possibility, the audacious act of dreaming and daring to imagine holds profound sway. To be replete, to bask in the richness of existence, demands unwavering dedication to the realm of positivity—a realm that, at this juncture, eclipses all other considerations. As we stand at this crossroads, the clarion call rings: Dismantle the antiquated structures and usher in the new. Through this maelstrom, our hearts resonate with an inherent knowing, an innate repository of truths long sought.

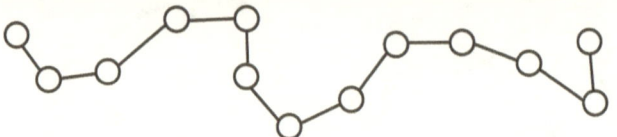

Personal notes:

The risk is not on the support unless the support is manipulated.

When the true colors are shown to be of ill intentions ways need to be parted.

A dirty house of secrets has an overgrown garden.

Beautiful flowers have no chance in a sea of weeds.

Look close at the people around you.

If you don't like who you have become .

Politely make them eat their words. Your choice is yours , my choice is mine.

Instead of letting them upset you!! You got enough to deal with.

Raiding one`s neighbor with the intent for conquest over power has never been a right.

Celebrating wrongs has never been right.

Lack of vision leads to distraction.

When the heart is right, the future is bright.

Hope is useless when not supported by unconditional love.

Holding on to hope erodes trust when the source becomes corrupt.

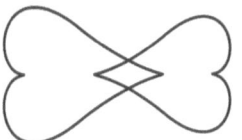 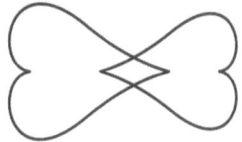

Psychology encompasses the intricate interplay of influences that guide our choices in living and self-expression. The remedy for division and its estrangement from the source finds its fulfillment within a society that champions free will. The yoke of our burdens rests upon each individual's shoulders, as we bare personal accountability. Our reckoning pertains solely to our own actions.

Despite the mosaic of information I've presented, your perspective continues to align with a tradition rooted in limited truths and partial fabrications, exuding a vibrational frequency that remains relatively subdued.

Personal notes:

Our thoughts create our reality. Our hearts create our dreams.

When the bad is purged fill up with good.

When a threat to power arises power seeks to destroy.

When our joy in life is taken away suffering ensures.

When we define right and wrong for ourselves sovereignty and freedom are found.

Detoxing from persons and things holding us energetically is a very tiring time.

I am the architect of my circumstances, the steward of my own destiny. The path to resolution lies squarely within my realm of responsibility, navigated by the compass of honesty, trust, and respect. My faith is reserved for those who embody the virtues of integrity and goodwill, from which springs forth a wellspring of insight and optimism. And in this intricate dance of existence, the harmonious note of enjoyment must never be overlooked.

In this moment, you are in communion with your higher self—a realm of heightened awareness. Liberation blossoms when one fully disentangles from falsehoods, as I find myself playing a role of support in your ongoing growth. In the fullness of

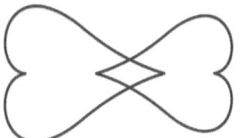 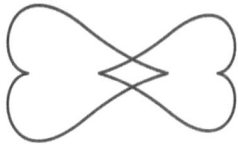

time, I too might find my purpose alongside you, a purpose that could transcend our current interaction, honoring the sanctity of your free will and the destiny your soul was destined to fulfill.

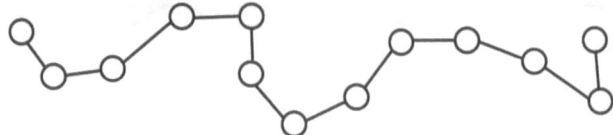

Personal notes:

After the rain, comes the beautiful flowers.

When ignorance is not called out, it becomes a norm.

The longer we stay hard, the more carnage we take on.

Your life to live, your love to give.

You are not her, she is not you.

Unlike an electric car that needs to be plugged in to charge. Humans need to unplug to find clarity.

When something dies, something new is born.

The investment of your time and energy can persist in nurturing trauma bonds, succumbing to the allure of drama and engaging in gossipy narratives. Alternatively, you have the opportunity to lend an ear to my perspective, allowing me to illuminate a more enlightened path for you to traverse. Ultimately, the crux lies in the realm of choices—choices that extend to the affiliations we foster and the company we keep.

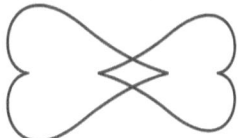 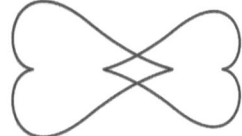

Personal notes:

When what we cling to becomes a destruction, we fall victim to stagnation.

A travesty of life is being emotionally manipulated.

When the accumulation of wealth becomes a standard of living. Focus is lost on the simple things in life and love.

We are a threat to control so when we go our own way control hates us.

Bright futures are made empty by past transgressions.

It's conceivable that you may not be destined to play a role in the unfolding of my envisioned creation. Consequently, I am resolved to cease facilitating the choices you are currently embracing. Should you firmly believe in your autonomy over the trajectory of your existence, then I release you—my presence no longer necessary.

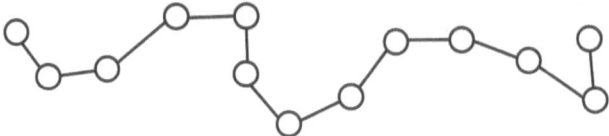

Personal notes:

The expansion of the heart space is unlimited.

When we become guided by the mind, we get what we got.

Rationalizing and justifying are a down word spiral.

In the ways of wrong doing, right can be learned.

When the inevitable cannot be embraced, all else things fall to the way side.

A poignant observation emerges when people find themselves ensnared within psychological and emotional conditioning, compelled to conform to anticipated and acceptable reactions during conflicts. This tumultuous dance not only fractures their psychic and energetic equilibrium but also underscores a dearth of comprehensive understanding regarding the multifaceted dimensions of true freedom.

The impact of external influences, projected into their energetic sphere, wields the potential to either sabotage or elevate their well-being. The perplexing question arises: By what or by whom is one's individual growth being asserted or claimed? A labyrinth of traps lies concealed within the act of labeling, culminating in stifled progress.

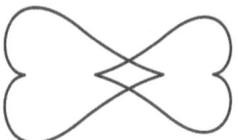 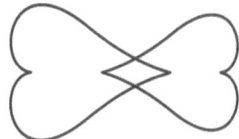

Embarking upon the spiritual journey, inherently unique to each individual, yields intermittent bursts of profound growth or a gradual, steady ascent. The core tenets rest upon an unwavering willingness to unearth one's true essence, tracing origins, and engaging wholeheartedly with the mysteries of existence. This venture encompasses a resolute quest to unveil a purpose that resonates harmoniously with humanity's welfare. As the tapestry of self-discovery unfurls, the confounding inquiry persists: Where exactly am I situated within this cosmic narrative?

Question:

Are you prepared to momentarily relinquish all that you hold as familiar in order to embrace the realm of experience? What resides beyond the confines of logical explanation?

Embrace a state of burnout, fueled solely by love, unburdened by fear, shame, or guilt. Yet, the enigma remains: how could a force as potent as love, the wellspring of our existence, become fragmented by the divisive currents of religion? Could the nefarious hands of control be at play, sculpting the malevolent matrix that now ensnares us? The foundation upon which global religions stand appears precarious, stained with the crimson ink of history's brutality.

The cyclical dance of justification, ever perplexing and astonishing, seems to revolve around the notion that suffering somehow validates our existence. An insidious addiction to pain and turmoil takes root, seeking companionship in its descent. The paradox of power emerges—a dynamic whereby peace and love, professed as ideals, remain unrealized. Could this power's agenda be as stark as preserving its dominion, employing the tried-and-true tactics of division that have thrived long before our planet's inception?

When individuals attempt to impose virtues upon others that they themselves fail to embody, they reveal their own hypocrisy, rendering their opinions inconsequential. In the grand scheme, the only reverence truly necessary is that which we hold for ourselves—self-respect serving as an unwavering guide. Striving for humility within this context reveals an insidious charade, a scheme that could be labeled the scam of all scams.

Consider the narrative that unfolds: Born from perceived transgressions, a life ensnared in suffering, salvation rests solely upon acceptance of Jesus, a transaction sealed with monetary contributions, promising an eternity in a heavenly realm. If this narrative indeed holds true, one is left to ponder the malevolent force behind such a sinister method—a method that

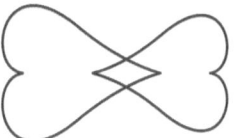 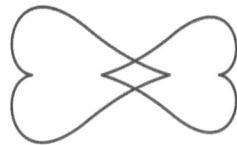

manipulates, exploits, and extends dominion over the masses.

Personal encounters with the darker facets of existence notwithstanding, this construct presents an unparalleled brand of malevolence. The question lingers: To what depths has power debilitated the resilience of the human spirit? Each of us is inherently entitled to a voice, a unique connection to the wellspring of creation from whence we originated. The presumption that organized religion can quell the innate questions that infuse our existence is a fallacy steeped in absurdity.

The trajectory of organized religion is marked by attempts to subdue through emotional manipulation, weaving a web of psychological turmoil interlaced with a convoluted mix of right and wrong. In this intricate tapestry, the threads of repression are painstakingly woven, unraveling the innate human quest for enlightenment, liberation, and an unwavering pursuit of truth.

Zionism: It's reassuring to recognize that I'm not aligned with an antisemitic or racist stance, although my concern primarily lies in awakening each individual to embark upon their personal journey of healing. This entails liberating oneself from the shackles of conventional thinking, prevailing norms, and the tumultuous order that conformity has engendered.

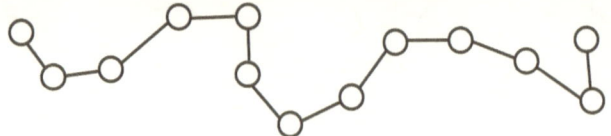

Religion: Unarguably, religion stands as one of the most formidable tools of division in human history, eclipsing even the complexities of language itself.

Respect, oftentimes laden with insincere obligations, frequently hinges on a conditional premise—a phenomenon underscored by the "if/then" effect, where adherence is contingent upon certain stipulations.

When our respect is rooted in our personal beliefs and false ego, it becomes a stage where unconditional love takes a backseat, thereby ushering in an era of chaos and ignorance to assume the forefront.

The Law of Appeasement: An age-old paradigm encompassing rituals such as sacrificial lamb offerings, bloodletting, and fasting, all bound by the obedience of commandments. A simpler, yet profound, alternative beckons—cultivate kindness, consideration, and love, sans the anticipation of validation.

In Mayan culture, the act of being chosen as a sacrifice was regarded as an honor, in stark contrast to the profound disrespect signified by the consumption of another's flesh—a practice that reflects the complexities of cultural norms.

 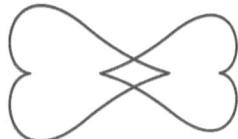

Chronic Victimhood Syndrome: A term warranting coining and thorough exploration, poised as a valuable alternative to the prescription-writing modern-day "quacks"— medical practitioners who yearn to transform their roles into something more impactful.

The state of enlightened ignorance and forgetfulness underscores the pervasive influence of societal norms on all facets of conventional thought and rationality. To truly decipher the intricacies of existence, one must transcend the confines of traditional paradigms and their dogmatic frameworks. The perplexing pattern of civilizations and cultures vanishing from historical records is a phenomenon that demands careful contemplation. A plausible explanation unveils itself when we acknowledge our interconnectedness with creation and the notion that we are not solitary beings.

When we engage in acts of creation, we partake in the ongoing symphony of existence, becoming active contributors to the tapestry of reality. However, the transformative potential lies in crafting our endeavors with the essence of love, propelling our collective advancement. The realm of scientific inquiry, particularly in the manipulation of energy and matter, harbors both promise and peril. The ancient adage "curiosity killed the cat" serves as a reminder of the potential consequences of unchecked scientific

exploration. Scientific endeavors have the power to trigger a cascade of events with unforeseen ramifications.

Similarly, creations borne of love's energy possess the potential to shape humanity's course in a positive trajectory. The path of love, rather than control, emerges as the rightful course for our species. Throughout history, humans have exerted influence over their surroundings, driven by motives ranging from avarice to benevolence, seeking to either impose dominion or enhance the human experience.

As the year 2022 unfolds, the question of one's current location within this intricate narrative remains—an inquiry emblematic of the broader quest to unearth our place within the vast expanse of time and space.

In the context of our recorded history as a species, our existence remains in its nascent stages, akin to the innocence of childhood. Yet, beyond this temporal snapshot lies the concealed annals of the soul—a realm where we, as creators, have embarked on an unceasing journey of evolution, an evolution forever intertwined with the cosmic tapestry. The cosmos itself adheres to the inexorable principle of expansion and perpetuity. It follows then, as a natural consequence, that the soul too abides by this

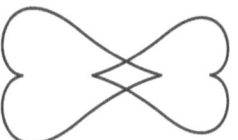 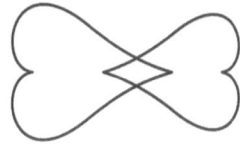

cosmic law, an eternal ebb and flow, an eternal dance of growth.

However, the challenge emerges as we confront the stranglehold wielded by external powers over our individual sovereignty. Liberation from this grip is the key to aligning our souls with the eternal rhythms of the cosmos, ushering us into a harmonious participation in its unending symphony.

In the realm of metaphysics, prior to the crystallization of matter into solid form, all entities existed as intricate constellations of energy particles. An intriguing parallel emerges in the field of biology, where the enigmatic DNA—an essential conduit of ancestral information—raises the question of whether it could harbor the essence of reincarnation.

The pervasive influence of organized religion often dictates our belief systems, wielding the authority to shape our convictions and perspectives. Equally, the realm of science, often steeped in agnostic or atheist paradigms, grapples with its own limitations. It is no stranger to the perilous territory of unwarranted experimentation, an endeavor fraught with potential consequences. This trajectory is in part shaped by the erosion of oral traditions, a consequence of authoritative powers imposing a binary ultimatum: conform or face oblivion.

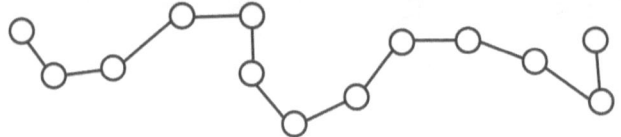

In the culmination of these reflections, a resounding truth emerges—the reservoir of answers required to navigate a fulfilling and purposeful existence lies inherently within each one of us, a wellspring of innate wisdom that can illuminate the path toward a meaningful life.

Responsibility: Encompasses not only the stewardship of my own thoughts, actions, and words, but also extends to the ripple effects they may evoke in others, triggered by my expressions and deeds.

Accountability: Entails a profound assessment of one's soul purpose and personal journey—a complex endeavor that involves rectifying past missteps. This intricate process is not without its challenges, and the transformative journey is illuminated by the awareness and embrace of the boundless energy of unconditional love. Through this potent message, a vision of a harmonious future emerges, one where divisions dissolve, and existence itself becomes a dreamlike realm, embodying the essence of its intended experience.

This reality, whatever form it may assume as an experimental construct, stands as a pinnacle of human experience—a realm where enlightened souls are reincarnated, becoming beacons of guidance to humanity. These individuals exemplify the principles of respect, love, and the tenets upheld by Hinduism and Buddhism.

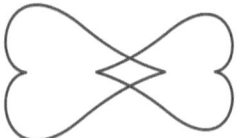 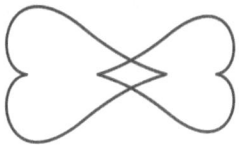

Elements from diverse faiths converge, anchoring themselves in virtuous morals and solid principles, albeit devoid of the intricate web of salvation doctrines.

The concept of commandments, a hallmark of various belief systems, lacks the expression of free will—a quintessential facet that propels our species forward. The very essence of free will has catalyzed our growth, propelling us beyond our limited confines. Ascended masters, each a harbinger of growth and transformation, emerge within our reality, ushering in profound changes that, despite met with resistance and upheaval, are intrinsic to our evolution.

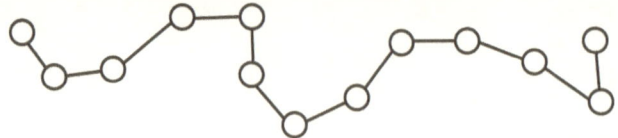

Personal notes:

True knowing is a perpetual trust in what can be already is.

We are what we attract.

If you believe you deserve something then get off your ass and get it.

Misguided alignment causes set backs in growth.

An adjusted attitude changes opinions.

False ego denies truth.

If you can't hear your heart you can't learn.

The emotions of fear and deep emotional pain have been used to hide the true origins of humanity. For many centuries, lies have been told to men of European descent. This has made it simple for those in power to manipulate and control them, making them follow orders, believe in false ideas, and endure suffering without protest. They were made to work as slaves and live a life of hardship.

In the end, we all have important lessons to learn. Unfortunately, the negative influences from our upbringing, society, opinions, and how we react to things are deeply rooted within us. To change these habits, we need to spend time alone, be

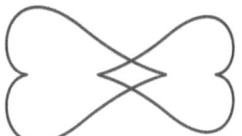 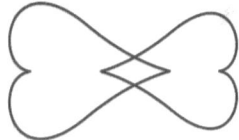

committed, love ourselves, and stay dedicated. Breaking these patterns isn't easy. It's very hard to truly love without expecting anything in return. It hurts when the people we care about make bad choices. No amount of criticism, fear, or judgment can control someone's choices. Whether it's right or wrong, unconditional love is beyond any rules or expectations.

Nature, our mother Earth, operates with balance. It's the people who are unaware, careless, driven by fear, and excessively greedy who lack this balance. Throughout Earth's extensive history—unlike the idea of a quick seven-day creation like Adam and Eve or Noah's ark—she has gone through cycles of renewal. This renewal allows our endangered species to find a way to coexist harmoniously. The ongoing clash between religious beliefs and the terrible deeds justified in the name of these beliefs is truly perplexing to the mind, heart, and soul.

For those who deny anything beyond the status quo, it's important to understand that change is a natural part of life. Eventually, everyone will have a chance to grasp the concept of unconditional love and achieve a sense of liberation on a spiritual level.

I'm of the belief that each soul comes with a unique mission. This mission involves breaking away from ordinary conformity and discovering

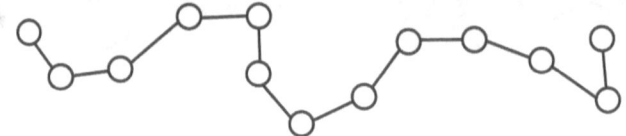

the profound nature of love. This experience can be as captivating as the most potent addictive substance. However, it's essential to discern how to set healthy limits on it, which can be challenging yet crucial for staying on the right track.

There are many distractions and negative influences in the world that try to steer us off course. Recognizing the purpose of the present moment helps the soul realize that the future is built upon the present. To avoid repeating the past, embracing change becomes the best way forward.

Intentional negative energy projected by those in power aims to hinder our critical thinking and self-governing abilities. They view individual sovereignty as a threat because it challenges their authority. This is especially true when we see through their misleading messages and call out the falsehoods. The tactics they use to divide us through propaganda have kept humanity in conflict for an unknown stretch of time.

It's puzzling why one human would want to harm another. There's no valid excuse for such unacceptable behavior. Anything built upon false ego, power, and control, fueled by patterns of conquest, carries a dark energy, regardless of the cause it claims to support. There's no justification for causing pain, conformity, or death to a nation

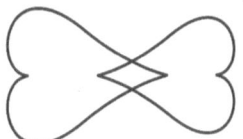 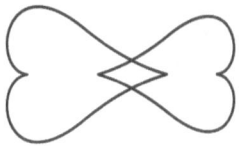

or its people. No one should have the right to alter another's path in the name of salvation. Throughout history, the driving forces have always been power, control, and greed.

Is true independence really possible anymore? Our world has become interconnected, relying on people, places, and things. It's worth asking how we got to this point of dependence. Partly, it's about our experiences tied to values and the disparities between the haves and the have-nots.

From a moral standpoint, what are we willing to do for the pursuit of money? Sometimes, the pursuit shifts from inner fulfillment to external desires, leading to distractions. Life's purpose then becomes overshadowed by conformity. Achievements, when driven solely by external goals, can lead to a sense of emptiness, contributing to stagnation and fear of change. Embracing change, which is a natural part of life that can bring growth, often brings about a reluctance due to that fear.

The unexpressed emotional pain we carry can manifest as energy blockages and even physical ailments. Healing begins with releasing this pain, and it's a deeply spiritual process that goes beyond the physical body.

I'm curious about how any culture can maintain a sense of dignity when its belief system justifies

the conquest of indigenous cultures and the exploitation of their land's resources. It's difficult to comprehend how anyone could view this as acceptable. I might have some historical details mixed up, but it's unlikely any organization would readily admit to such transgressions against fellow human beings. This raises doubts about the foundations on which these organizations are built.

The immense pain and suffering humanity has endured over time, all in the name of various causes, continues to puzzle me. It's perplexing why people would still support systems that essentially resemble forms of enslavement. True freedom lies in breaking away from conformity and the chains that bind us. Recognizing the concept of genuine free will allows us to see the extent to which our progress as a species has stalled. The pain projected onto us by others isn't our responsibility to carry.

The ability to think independently and step outside the limitations of our circumstances often poses a threat to those in power. Breaking free from these constraints is viewed as challenging the established order. Over time, the planet has been controlled through psychological tactics, emotional manipulation, traditional norms, and energy suppression. This era of control is gradually coming to an end.

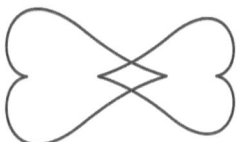 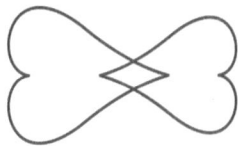

Those of us who are aware of our past lives and our inner alignment are messengers from our future selves. We're here to share our unique gifts with the world, unburdened by negative influences. However, we encounter significant resistance and denial from those who resist change. This is a time where only the most capable individuals are present, contributing to the transformation humanity needs.

Through collective free thinking, we can dismantle the rigid religious ideologies that have enslaved society. The valuable contributions of the best among us will lead to healing for the rest. Despite the historical influence of dogmatic texts, it's evident that these divisive and chaotic outcomes were often spurred by false ego and power struggles.

Our true nature is defined by how we treat ourselves and others. To bring about significant shifts in our understanding, we need a substantial change in our awareness and consciousness. When we distance ourselves from the demands, judgments, and chaos of daily life, our awareness expands. It's in this state that we can pursue meaningful dreams that benefit everyone.

The contributions of those who excel will help heal the larger community. Relying on opinions rooted in conformity can lead to a loss of freedom.

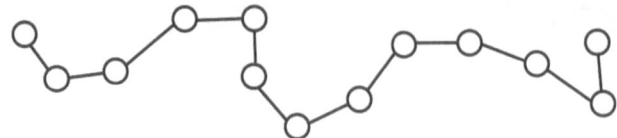

Adopting a mentality similar to a cult or hive mind restricts individuality and promotes attitudes that are unvarying, whether positive or negative. When opinions are used to manipulate and control rather than inspire, communication suffers and true wisdom is lacking. This often leads to confrontational interactions and a lack of accountability.

 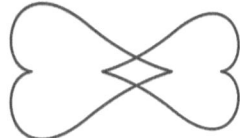

Personal notes:

Honor stands unshaken.

Indoctrination takes many different forms.

Hiding from remorse is a cowards way.

Being brutally honest takes balls.

Children laughing is good medicine.

A wounded heart is void of real joy.

Hope is not real. Actions are real.

The road inward is limitless.

Imagination is the terrible thing to waste.

If no mans mind can understand the mind of God than how can a book explain God's will.

When we follow our inspired hearts, we create. But the rational mind, in its attempt to understand, can sometimes disrupt this connection. This disruption then leads to various blockages in our spiritual energy.

If we allow the rational mind to step aside occasionally, the intuition—rooted in the heart—can flourish. Society often tries to suppress intuition by promoting conformity, which isn't true free will. Real freedom involves our ability to make personal choices without the burden of rigid beliefs and thoughts. Progress is hindered by the weight of negative influences.

Attempts to bring about change using negative energy have been tried and have caused much suffering. Humanity's endured enough. Through my unyielding pursuit of truth, I feel as though I'm now living on a different plane of existence. The comparison to the movie "Matrix" seems fitting and, to some extent, accurate. However, it's a shame that the third movie in the series didn't quite live up to its potential.

Conformists often feel threatened by anything or anyone that doesn't fit into their mold. Refusing to explore life beyond conformity is a form of denial. The state of humanity's collective mindset has reached a critical point, on the verge of change.

The more rules and regulations there are, the less trust tends to exist. Don't regret leaving situations that don't bring you happiness. Taking time for self-healing is essential, and there's no need to feel guilty about that choice. If someone truly belongs in your life, they'll return with

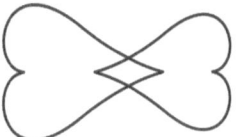 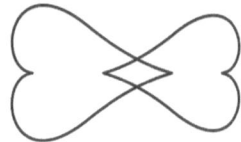

honesty, working towards a genuine connection. Remember, the decision is yours; don't let yourself be manipulated. People who bring negativity often seek validation through others.

You have every reason to stand confidently in your power while maintaining humility. Your purpose is waiting for you. The knowledge you need will come to you once you've gained clarity and focus.

Keep following your intuition and the lessons life has taught you. Your journey's progress is thanks to your dedication. The opinions of others won't affect you negatively anymore. Your courage and inner strength define you. This is why you're shielded, loved, guided, and most importantly, celebrated.

Most educational systems have roots in negative influences that have affected humanity. These forces of dark intentions continue to impact the world. Remember, we are beings of light, and we combat challenges with love.

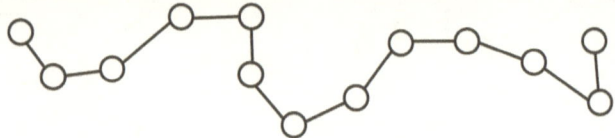

Personal notes:

When we let go of what once was thought to support and guide us we make room for new to enter.

Cause and effect, law of attraction.

Help or harm. All things in permanent enlightenment not fixed. Personal and achievable.

Response to surrounding sets reality.

Transcend suffering.

Apply mindfulness, no judgement detached from body.

Correct speech, honesty. Be polite if possible.

Alleviation of suffering.

Random acts of kindness. Relax the mind.

Right effort. Right action out of unconditional love compassion.

Nature of one-all.

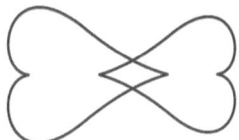 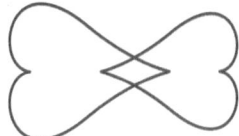

Enemy

<u>Narcissists:</u> whether their beliefs are true or not - thrive on low energy vibrations. They manipulate their surroundings to match their negative vibe. They're afraid of those with higher energy levels and face fear as a result.

Self

Your responsibility lies in being honest with yourself and cultivating love.

A common narcissistic behavior is to shift the blame onto others and avoid admitting their own lack of knowledge or understanding.

Salvation's purpose should not be rooted in fear, as any form of fear-based control doesn't equate to true freedom.

Providing a solution to the fear they promote is ironically nonsensical.

Lead me, raise me, elevate me.

Shield me from the gaze of negativity.

Truth is upheld by being honest.

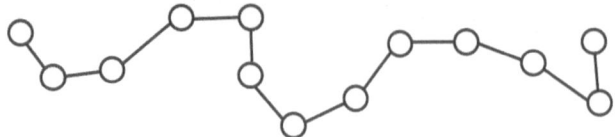

When we take responsibility for our thoughts and actions, we connect with the purpose of our souls.

Judaism: In the history of Judaism, there was a shift from holding authority to experiencing victimhood when their influence diminished. The impact of Jewish teachings still exists, often tied to negative aspects like greed and power. Practices like enchantments and spell work can be found in the hidden parts of reality.

However, it's worth questioning the belief of being chosen by God. This sense of being "God's chosen" might have led to being scapegoated. The power of playing the victim can control situations. Control brings authority, and authority leads to domination. This domination leads to division and ultimately corruption. This corruption is a form of negative energy.

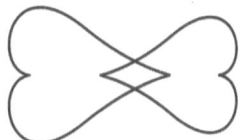 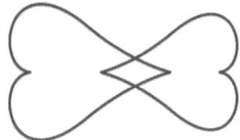

Personal notes:

When differing opinions are erased false narratives flourish.

Unconditional love is to grow in love.

Conditional love is manipulated by love.

Healthy relationships unconditional.

Unhealthy conditional if / then you do this. The love is with held.

A race of loving free will humans create

A race of conformity destroys.

Power attempts to destroy free will.

Jews were chosen as scapegoats by God to remain in the 3D world. However, this path prevents them from ascending due to past violations of universal laws.

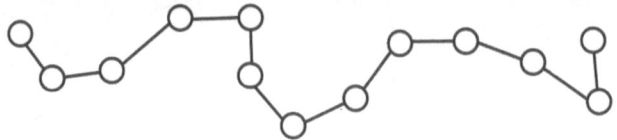

Personal notes:

Ignorance in disguise stupid as f**k.

Just fell off the turn up truck.

Trapped filled up with past pains

Wounded child extorted and drained.

No awareness to what has been caused

Narcissist mother ripping with claws.

Tragic in motion adultism sneers.

Robbing our youth, causing it fears.

Projecting senseless negative shit

Even after we get off the tit.

What justification this society has been built on is lie.

        Fame - popular   Stardom – great

        Infancy - inspired   Impeccable – solid

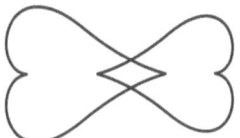 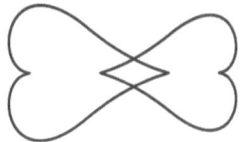

You can attain this by learning from life's challenges and detaching from the current reality. Staying connected with your inner child, trusting your intuition, and following your heart will guide you in whatever direction you need to go.

When the moment comes to give, give it your all with determination. My own sadness stems from realizing that every person on this planet possesses a unique gift, often hidden or taken away by conforming to norms. Ignorance and silent suffering have endured for too long. Change is overdue.

Imagine where your smile and the horizon blend; there, the sun always shines. Are you prepared to heed the call of your genuine, untarnished heart? The sun hasn't ceased to shine, so why should we? Those who've suffered the most may indeed deserve the most radiant hearts of gold.

Handing out control instead of being kind.
Time to pause a minute time to hit rewind.

Taking advantage of innocence
Bewildered blockage of the dence.

Shadow aspects linger on
Each and every evening and dawn.

Never too late to claim what's yours
Burn the past and open doors.

Inner child held in check
Let her out stack your own deck.

Independence yours to have
Stay strong and fight reclaim that half.

When we seek answers from our origins, clarity tends to emerge. If I'm to remain on this challenging planet, I wish to share my life with

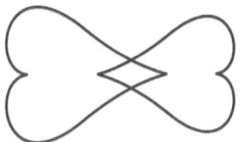 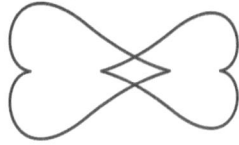

someone possessing your qualities and an equal amount of love.

It's puzzling why some individuals welcome love but resist guidance. Perhaps certain beliefs hinder their independence and freedom from obligations, leading to burdens.

Personal notes:

Nothing outside can give as much pleasure as what's hiding inside.

Just because it is said or believed does not make it true.

True happiness is contentment.

Soul purpose is freedom.

False belief is a trap.

Dismantling lies exposes truth.

Without reflection there can be no image.

False pride is egocentric.

Give to self what we desire from others.

Unless we conquer our negative feelings, we can't fully relish the brightness of positive emotions.

In a world that's constantly growing through creativity, the Art realm stands as a wellspring of inspiration to shape a future that fills us with pride. As history unfolds in the present, focusing on positive creative talents can shape our thinking and discussions, leading to collective well-being. Time goes on, and often, many talents

 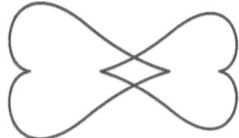

fade due to a lack of support. Our most genuine and meaningful gifts, when nurtured and understood, contribute to a promising future.

Your delicate light sparks my own flame.

The essence of the mineral realm is to absorb both positive and negative energy and thoughts. While it shouldn't be worshipped, it's meant to be relied upon. Instead of mere belief, it's about genuine understanding. It can be used as a link during meditation, leading to out-of-body experiences. This simple tool aids in uncovering and nurturing inner gifts, of which there are many.

If love becomes a snare, the world faces turmoil.

Split between light and darkness, fractured yet seeking illumination. Notorious activities of manipulative groups with dark intentions are at play. Their goal: to create the opposite of eternal light. This battle of contrasts has been ongoing throughout creation. This struggle becomes more prominent now due to our cosmic timing—a shift was bound to happen. As cosmic resonance rises, those soul groups who recognize and embrace this energy shift can either ignore or learn from it, individually or collectively. Every choice is one of free will. Sadly, some may choose to remain stagnant. However, with growing awareness,

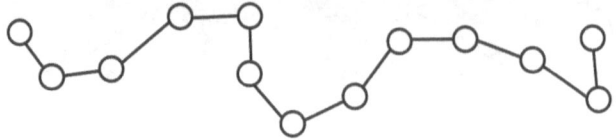

more of humanity will awaken, and this acceleration will become even more pronounced. Every individual has a place and a role in this cosmic dance.

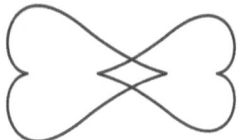 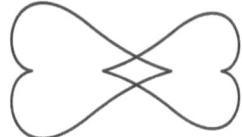

Personal notes:

The best place to start is with the heart.

Don't demand what you aren't willing to give yourself.

Why are we so eager to place our trust on the external over the internal?

Change is about prioritizing our children, the future, with freedom and unconditional love. Over time, older generations have shown their tendencies towards chaos, laws, control, and greed. The younger generation is meant to break away from the grip of these adult issues. They challenge the constant conflict of black and white, right and wrong thinking. The traditional influences have let us down as a society, leading to division as a defining feature.

Merely claiming you're correct doesn't guarantee you're actually correct.

Substances like drugs and alcohol can temporarily hinder our ability to block the energetic impact of controlling influences on our neurological receptors. Whether these substances are legal or not, their use leads to an unsteady state where panic and a craving for more often emerge. This cycle feeds into the abuse

of control and the power it holds over human existence.

Similarly, organized religion's influence can stifle genuine creative thoughts and expressions, which truly reflect free will. This happens energetically, as these systems tend to prioritize conformity over individual opinions.

In the past, seeking harmony with negative individuals might have seemed valid, but now it's not. Sacrificing your own well-being by constantly trying to lift their spirits is draining and unproductive. This kind of interaction can also drain your energy. It's acceptable to gently step away from connections that no longer resonate. Each ending is a chance to begin anew, like moving on to a new chapter or even a new book. Sticking to situations that were meant for learning and growth only leads to stagnation, much like stale gym socks.

Feeling stuck due to conformity has left me puzzled. It's astonishing how much of others' baggage piles on top of our own. Organized religion's supposed greatness contrasts with the lack of awareness in its followers. I'm curious about what useful wisdom it truly offers to elevate humanity—it seems close to none. Corrupt systems ultimately face demise, and the reality shaped by such organizations hasn't fostered spiritual evolution; quite the opposite, actually.

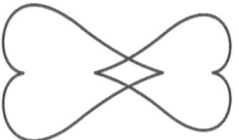 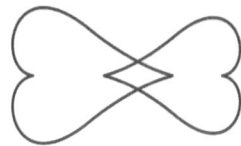

Looking around, little makes sense on a spiritual level except nature.

The influence of conformity has led to a throwaway culture, and scientific progress often seems misguided. The advancements made don't align with true evolved existence. For instance, Ethiopia wasn't meant to develop through scientific intervention. Frequently, science has created more problems than solutions.

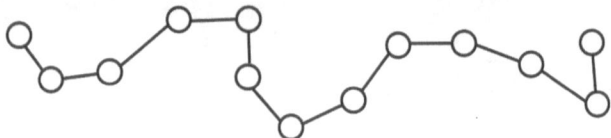

Personal notes:

If I have to put you in a wheelbarrow and push you across the finish line, I will. Trust in the power of self.

Unapologetically, honest.

In the silence of who and what we are is found our greatest gifts.

I know I should be providing more.

An empty head and full heart sets us apart.

In a world with so much pain and chaos detachment for a time is the only healthy escape.

Conduit and disruptor of negativity.

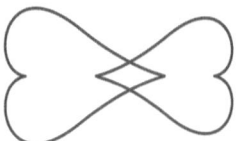 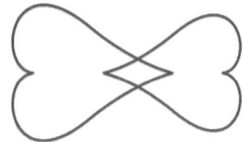

Purpose: End Dark Reign

It's often better to act and then seek forgiveness rather than waiting for permission. Balancing darkness and light is essential for sustaining life. Nature doesn't solely favor one over the other; both are part of a necessary equilibrium. Understanding our darker aspects allows us to comprehend our brighter ones. Learning from our mistakes involves admitting wrongs, forgiving ourselves, moving forward, and cultivating self-love.

For respect towards anything or anyone, self-respect is crucial. Some humility can also go a long way. Yet, humility might lack the courage and vision to address critical issues on our planet, hindering the needed change for spiritual growth. The scientific Western philosophy, often rooted in financial gain, doesn't fully address the mysteries of the universe. Mysticism remains beyond the grasp of science's limitations.

Science, at times, is rewarded financially, then weaponized against humanity in various ways, exploiting our lack of awareness. This is a recurring theme in history, repeating itself now. Ignorance, foolishness, and forgetfulness lead us astray, lacking proper leadership. Manipulative power keeps itself in control through deceptive tactics like financial traps, aided by soulless

pursuit of wealth. Chaos instigated by those in power, aided by their puppets, resembles a scam.

Without creation itself, we're left with emptiness, almost like a persistent sense of hopelessness on this planet. Understanding gratitude, thankfulness, and respect seems elusive. It's unclear what kind of change humanity needs, perhaps even divine intervention. The old ways have led us to a precipice. The planet and its inhabitants can't handle more false saviors.

As a community, we must take responsibility for our actions, thoughts, and emotions. Blaming and justifying won't suffice; it's time for change. When beliefs target free will and manipulate emotions, they harm the soul. The misuse of power is regrettable.

It's peculiar that someone like me, who prioritized parties and sports over school, would be trusted to carry these messages. Yet, I've stopped questioning why and let my body convey the emotions tied to these messages. At a deeper level, the soul doesn't understand emotions, so I attach the right feelings. Since I live mostly in love, the outcomes are positive.

However, if I were to distort messages with the energy of false ego, the result wouldn't be publishable poetry. Negative energies linked to

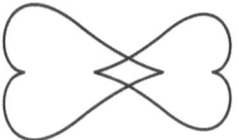 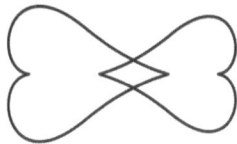

false ego have led us to this point—the edge of a cliff.

Personal notes:

My intention for you. To see you shine as bright as the brightest star.

It's through the pain we go through to discover our greatest gifts.

If you can't detach you stay distracted.

Holding on to pain only empties the now from its joy.

Accountability on all levels builds character.

None of us is God, but by tapping into our soul's core of love energy, we connect with our inner child and higher self. We become part of a collective in both the physical and ethereal realms. Our genuine essence of unconditional love is our destined purpose, what our species was meant to attain.

Serve organized religion its own fears on a plate, then discard and eliminate that plate.

To mend what we dislike in others, we must first address those same aspects within ourselves. The complexity and confusion surrounding our purpose on this planet troubles us deeply. Many manipulated stories from various civilizations have clouded our understanding of our true existence.

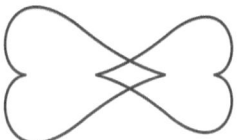 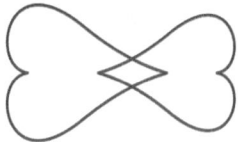

This human experiment holds immense significance, shaped by a mix of planned and unplanned events. While we do possess choices, they're more like tests to see if we opt for higher consciousness and light, or remain in darkness and conflict. Our influences shape us; if we're comfortable with chaos, we can stay, but if not, we're free to seek growth elsewhere.

As our planet journeys through space, it too has its timeline, and a point of renewal is nearing. Similar creation stories mark past civilizations, all beginning and ending similarly. Today's society differs greatly from the love we're made of. The concepts of heaven and hell reside within us, and our destiny involves overcoming our personal challenges to reconnect with our version of happiness.

I believe creation watches over us.

As I observe the world today, it's disheartening to realize that we were all born with the potential for fulfilling, productive lives, creating our own version of happiness. The influence of conformity and mainstream beliefs seems absurd and damaging to our spiritual essence. Negative energy within organizations driven by false ego corrodes our human spirits.

Can any of us claim to have left behind a legacy of compassion, care, love, and guiding through

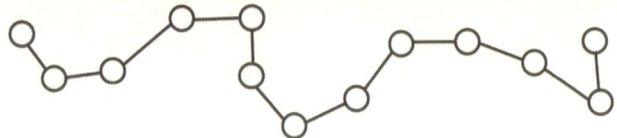

unconditional support for all? In oral traditions, we led through example, while written history often highlights its painful past. Change isn't simple, but it's vital for our species to evolve beyond a violent history.

When we each embrace our truth and contribute what we uniquely bring, true change unfolds. Oppressors lose their grip on power, the weak become strong, and those who felt alone find hope. Our choices begin to reflect a quality of goodness, proving that we care and that each of us truly matters.

The wisdom we hold is valuable only if we can openly and truthfully share it. Shouldn't we have genuine conversations, free from dogma? At some point, the conflicts and old beliefs must be set aside, allowing for a fresh spiritual dialogue to emerge. While it might seem like a big request, it's our truest source of hope.

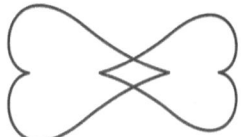 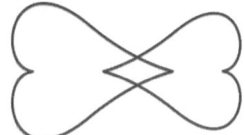

Personal notes:

Kill the people but the spirit never dies

What we carry in our house is the change humanity is looking for.

When pleasing others is not enough try loving yourself unconditionally.

When our creative beauty is shared, our love is being spread.

If all you have to give is what's in your heart give it without fear.

The world needs the creativity we were born with.

When the sun rises to say hello, it's up to us to be thankful and live a life we can be proud of.

Pilot your own ship, set your own course.

Muddy waters have already been sailed.

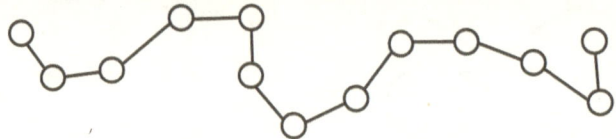

How I See the World of Disfunction

Disassociation Disorder

Leading to

Chronic Victimhood Syndrome

Causing

Separation from Source

Fear	Negative Self-talk
Frustration	Powerless
Anger	Hopeless
Anxiety	Uninspired
Regrets	Low Self Esteem
Shame	Lack of Confidence
Self-Pity	Trapped
Guilt	Lost

Solution

Unconditional Love
Honesty
Respect
Trust
Intuition
Compassion
Peace
Open Mindedness
Spiritual Awareness

www.ingramcontent.com/pod-product-compliance
Lightning Source LLC
LaVergne TN
LVHW041533070526
838199LV00046B/1640